Blender 2D Animation

Blender, the 3D modeling and animation program, is a free, open-source, 3D, computer graphics software toolset used for creating animated films, visual effects, art, 3D printed models, motion graphics, interactive 3D applications, virtual reality and computer games. Grease Pencil is a component of Blender. *Blender 2D Animation: The Complete Guide to the Grease Pencil, Second Edition* describes how to access the Grease Pencil component in Blender and create 2D animation within the Blender 3D environment. It is assumed that the reader has no previous knowledge of the Blender program, and the text treats 2D animation using the Grease Pencil as a standalone application.

Key Features

- A comprehensive beginner's guide to the Grease Pencil component of Blender facets of operation is explained in short, concise chapters with cross references.
- Written instruction is accompanied by diagram illustrations in reference to the program's Graphical User Interface.
- The text is also available in a discounted set along with *The Complete Guide to Blender Graphics: Computer Modeling & Animation*.

John M. Blain has become a recognised expert in Blender, having authored to date eight successful prior editions of *The Complete Guide to Blender Graphics*. He became enthused with Blender upon retirement from a career in mechanical engineering. The original book came from personal notes compiled in the course of self-learning. The notes were recognised as an ideal instruction source by Neal Hirsig, Senior Lecturer (retired) at Tufts University. Mr. Hirsig encouraged publication of the first edition and in doing so is deserving of the author's gratitude. Gratitude must also be extended to the author's wife Helen for her continuing encouragement and patience as new editions of the book are compiled.

Blender 2D Animation
The Complete Guide to the Grease Pencil
Second Edition

John M. Blain

CRC Press
Taylor & Francis Group
Boca Raton London New York

CRC Press is an imprint of the
Taylor & Francis Group, an **informa** business

AN A K PETERS BOOK

Designed cover image: Cover art available to share and use under the Creative Commons Attribution ShareAlike license (CCBY-SA 3.0).
Attribution: Blender Foundation – www.blender.org
Artists: Daniel Martinez Lara, Javier Salvador, Maria Vela, Sergi Miranda

Second edition published 2024
by CRC Press
6000 Broken Sound Parkway NW, Suite 300, Boca Raton, FL 33487-2742

and by CRC Press
4 Park Square, Milton Park, Abingdon, Oxon, OX14 4RN

CRC Press is an imprint of Taylor & Francis Group, LLC

First edition published by AK Peters 2021

Library of Congress Cataloging-in-Publication Data

Names: Blain, John M., 1942- author.
Title: Blender 2D animation : the complete guide to the Grease pencil /
John M. Blain.
Other titles: Grease pencil 2D animation
Description: 2nd edition. | Boca Raton, FL : CRC Press, [2024] | Includes
bibliographical references and index.
Identifiers: LCCN 2023058985 (print) | LCCN 2023058986 (ebook) | ISBN
9781032631479 (hbk) | ISBN 9781032649795 (pbk) | ISBN 9781032649832
(ebk)
Subjects: LCSH: Computer animation. | Blender (Computer file) | Grease
pencil.
Classification: LCC TR897.72.B55 B524 2024 (print) | LCC TR897.72.B55
(ebook) | DDC 777/.7--dc23/eng/20240131
LC record available at https://lccn.loc.gov/2023058985
LC ebook record available at https://lccn.loc.gov/2023058986

ISBN: 978-1-0326-3147-9 (hbk)
ISBN: 978-1-0326-4979-5 (pbk)
ISBN: 978-1-0326-4983-2 (ebk)

DOI: 10.1201/9781032649832

Typeset in ArilMT
by KnowledgeWorks Global Ltd.

Publisher's note: This book has been prepared from camera-ready copy provided by the authors.

Blender Grease Pencil 2D Animation

Contents

Blender Grease Pencil 2D Animation

Blender 2D and the Book

This book describes how to access the **Grease Pencil** component in **Blender** and create **2D Animation** within the Blender 3D environment. It is assumed that the reader has no previous knowledge of the Blender program and treats **2D Animation** using the **Grease Pencil** as a stand alone application.

The **Grease Pencil** is a component of the **3D Modeling and Animation Program - Blender**.

Blender is a **free open-source 3D Computer Graphics software tool set** used for creating animated films, visual effects, art, 3D printed models, motion graphics, interactive 3D applications, virtual reality and computer games.

Blender supports the entirety of the 3D pipeline—modeling, rigging, animation, simulation, rendering compositing and motion tracking, video editing and the **2D Animation Pipeline**.

The Blender program is maintained by the **Blender Foundation** and released as **Open Source Software** which is available for download and **FREE** to be used for any purpose.

The first step in using the Grease Pencil, is to download, install and open Blender. These operations are described in separate sections.

The second step is accessing the **Grease Pencil** when Blender is running. This step is often overlooked in many tutorials and requires explanation.

When Blender is opened, it opens in 3D Modeling Mode. The instruction in this book will, therefore, begin by briefly describe the 3D Interface to establish the basic concept of operation.

The **Grease Pencil** was originally a Tool for drawing construction notes during the 3D Modeling and Animation process. This Tool still exists but has been developed to facilitate 2D Drawing and Animation. 3D Modelling and Animation in Blender takes place in a 3D Workspace which is the arrangement of panels or windows in the programs interface. For 2D Animation a separate **Workspace** (arrangement of panels) has been developed which resides within the 3D environment.

Program Development

This book has been compiled using **Blender Version 3.5.3** and checked against the imminent release of **Blender 4.0.0**.

Be aware, **Blender** is continually evolving as developments which expand and improve functionality are added. Developments are introduced frequently which often incur subtle changes and modifications to operational procedures and to the program's display. When this occurs, Blender is released with a **New Version Number**.

When attempting Blender for the first time by following a tutorial, whether it is a book, a written tutorial or a video tutorial, always consider the Blender version for which the tutorial is written and work through examples using that version of Blender. It is tempting to grab the latest Blender release but consider the information given, in the tutorial, as a training exercise then step up to the latest developments in the current version. Blender maintains a download page containing all earlier releases of the program (see Download and Installation).

2D Animation Concept

One example of 2D Animation is depicted in the **Walk Cycle** where drawings of a character in different poses are displayed in quick succession creating the illusion of the character walking.

Grease Pencil Animation Example

To see an example of 2D Animation created using Blender's Grease Pencil see:

HERO – Blender Grease Pencil Showcase
at
https://www.youtube.com/watch?v=pKmSdY56VtY

Grease Pencil Definition from Wikipedia

The **grease pencil**, is a wax writing tool also known as a **wax pencil**, **china marker**, or **chinagraph pencil**, which is a writing implement made of hardened colored wax and is useful for marking on hard, glossy non-porous surfaces. Marks made by grease pencils are resistant to moisture and can usually be removed by rubbing the marked surface with a paper towel.

So why Blender Grease Pencil?

When using Blender to construct 3D Scenes and generate animations it has been useful for artists to sketch notes on the computer screen. This does not mean that a crayon, as described above, was employed but that a digital marking was superimposed on the work being created. This marking is drawn on a separate digital layer which is easily modified or removed when the work is finished.

Sketching freehand notes is accomplished by drawing Strokes (lines), therefore, the concept has been developed to drawing sketches of characters and scenery as depicted in a cartoon drawing. Further development has seen the lines forming the sketch animated thus creating full 2D Animation. This 2D Animation, in Blender, is constructed within the Blender 3D environment providing a flexible animation tool. The tool has been termed, the **Grease Pencil** and is applied within a dedicated **2D Animation Workspace**.

A **Workspace** is the arrangement of panels and windows containing controls as seen on the computer screen when the program is run.

To understand this concept, begin by downloading and installing Blender.

To follow the instructions provided in this book it is suggested that you employ **Blender 3.5.3.**

Philosophy of the Book

The philosophy employed in this publication is to introduce **Blender** by describing the program's **Graphical User Interface (GUI)** and give short descriptions and examples of the controls and their function. The Controls constitute the Tools for performing the different operations which produce specific results. Knowing what Tools are available and where they are located is the key to understanding Blender.

Blender Platforms

A **computing platform** or **digital platform** is the environment in which a piece of software is executed. It may be the hardware or the operating system (OS).

Blender is a cross-platform application for **Windows Vista and above, Linux** and **Mac OSX 10.6** and above operating systems.

System Requirements

Graphics

Blender 2.82 and later requires OpenGL 3.3 or above, with recent graphics drivers from your graphics card manufacturer.

Hardware

Minimum (basic usage) hardware

- 64-bit dual core 2Ghz CPU with SSE2 support.
- 4 GB RAM
- 1280×768 display
- Mouse, Trackpad or Pen plus Tablet
- Graphics Card with 1 GB RAM, OpenGL 3.3
- Less than 10 years old.

Recommended hardware

- 64-bit quad core CPU
- 16 GB RAM
- Full HD display
- Three-button mouse or pen plus tablet
- Graphics card with 4 GB RAM

Optimal (production-grade) hardware

- 64-bit eight core CPU
- 32 GB RAM
- Full HD displays
- Three button mouse and pen plus tablet
- Graphics card with +12 GB RAM
-

Supported Graphics Cards

- **NVIDIA**: GeForce 400 and newer, Quadro Tesla GPU architecture and newer, including RTX-based cards, with NVIDIA drivers (list of all GeForce and Quadro GPUs)

- **AMD**: GCN 1st gen and newer. Since Blender 2.91, Terascale 2 architecture is fully depreciated, try using 2.90 (albeit not supported, it might still work) [list of all AMD GPUs]

- **Intel**: Haswell and newer (list of all Intel GPUs)
- **macOS**: Version 10.13 or newer with supported hardware.

Preamble

Before reading this book it will help if you are aware of the way in which it is written and the conventions employed.

Formats Conventions and Commands

In writing this book the following format conventions have been adopted:

Paragraphs are separated by an empty line and have not been indented.

Key words and phrases are printed in **bold text** with the first letter of a component name specific to Blender capitalized. **Bold text**, therefore, replaces the use of inverted commas.

Headings are printed in **Bold Olive Green.**

The following conventions will be used when giving instructions.

When using a Mouse connected to a computer, the commands will be:

Click or **Click LMB** – In either case this means make a single click with the left mouse button with the Mouse Cursor positioned over a control displayed on the computer Screen. In some instances it is explicit that the left mouse button should be used.

A Control – Is a designated area on the computer Screen represented by an icon in the form of a button or bar, with or without text annotation.

Double Click – Make two clicks in quick succession with **LMB** (the left mouse button).

Click, Hold and Drag – Click the left mouse button; hold it depressed while moving the mouse. Release the button at the end of the movement.

Click RMB – Click the right mouse button.

Click MMB – Click the middle mouse button (the middle mouse button may be the scroll wheel).

Scroll MMB – Scroll (rotate) the scroll wheel (MMB).

Clicking is used in conjunction with placing the Mouse Cursor over a button, icon or a slider which is displayed on the Screen.

Drawing Strokes (Lines) – The initial introduction to drawing Strokes will be demonstrated using a Mouse.

How to use a Drawing Tablet with a Stylus will follow.

Book Illustration

When the Blender program opens the interface displays in a dark color scheme. The scheme is appropriately named **Blender Dark.**

Blender Dark is one of several color schemes which you may choose or you can customize the interface to your personal preferences.

The illustrations in this book have, by and large, been constructed using screen captures taken with the Blender interface in one of the alternative color schemes named **Blender Light.**

Blender Dark	**Blender Light**

To view the Blender interface in the **Blender Light Theme**, have Blender opened (see Chapter 17) then in the upper left-hand corner of the Screen click with the Left Mouse button on Edit, drag the Mouse down placing the Cursor over Preferences and click LMB.

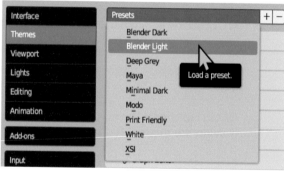

In the Blender Preferences panel which opens click on Themes in the left-hand column and where you see **Blender Dark** at the top of the right-hand column, place the Mouse Cursor over Blender Dark and click with the left Mouse button. Select (click) on **Blender Light** in the menu that displays.

Close the Blender Preferences panel by clicking on the cross in the upper right-hand corner of the panel.

The next time you open Blender the interface will display in the **Blender Light** Theme.

1

Introducing
The Grease Pencil

1.1 Blender and the Grease Pencil

The **Grease Pencil** is a component of Blender.

Blender is a computer **3D Modeling and Animation** program.

When Blender is opened, it displays on the computer monitor or screen with an arrangement of Panels or Windows which constitute a **Workspace**. The Panels in Blender are referred to as **Editors**.

The arrangement of Editors that display when Blender is first run is the default Workspace designed for 3D Modeling and Animation.

The first step to **2D Animation using Blender's Grease Pencil** is to activate the **2D Workspace** which is the **2D Drawing Environment** in Blender (Figure 1.1a).

Blender 3D Modeling and Animation   Figure 1.1a

Blender Default Screen   **Splash Screen Removed**

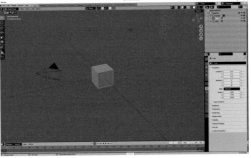

Grease Pencil 2D Animation Workspace

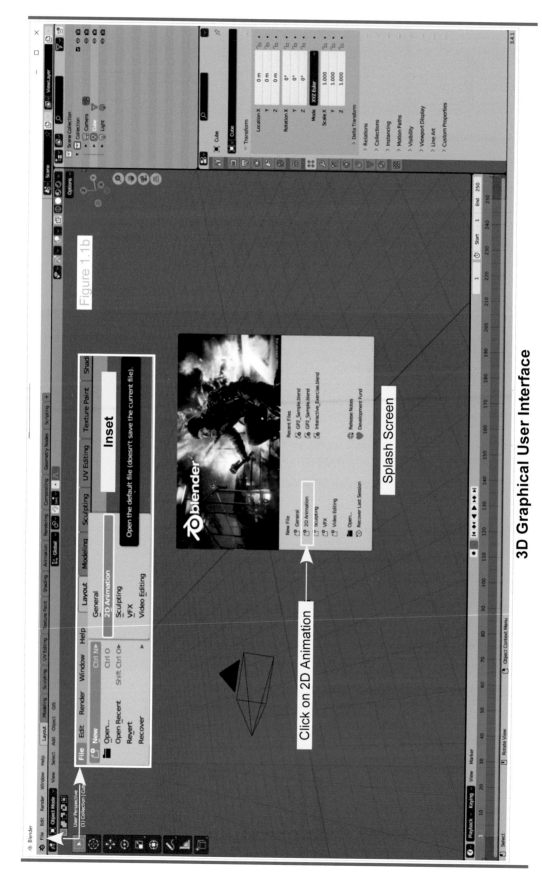

Figure 1.1b

3D Graphical User Interface

1.2 Activating the 2D Environment

It will be assumed that you have downloaded and installed the Blender program and that you have the program opened displaying the **Graphical User Interface** on your computer Screen (Figure 1.1b).

If you are new to Blender and require assistance in downloading, installing and opening Blender please see **Chapter 17** towards the end of the book.

With Blender opened you see the **Graphical User Interface (GUI)** as shown in Figure 1.1b opposite.

The **Graphical User Interface** is the arrangement of panels or windows making up a **Workspace**. There are different Workspaces for different functions.

When Blender is first opened it displays the **3D Modeling Workspace** with the **Splash Screen** superimposed in the center of the Screen. The Splash Screen only displays when Blender is first opened and if you click with the Mouse anywhere in the interface the Splash Screen disappears.

To activate the **2D Environment** (**2D Workspace**) click with the **Left Mouse Button** (LMB) in the Splash Screen where you see **2D Animation** (Figure 1.1b).

Alternatively, if the Splash Screen has been cancelled, LMB mouse over on **File** at the top left of the Screen, LMB Click, drag the Mouse Cursor over **New** then over **2D Animation** and **Click LMB** on **2D Animation** (see Figure 1.1b inset).

The Screen changes to the **2D Animation Workspace** which is **The Grease Pencil** (Figure 1.2).

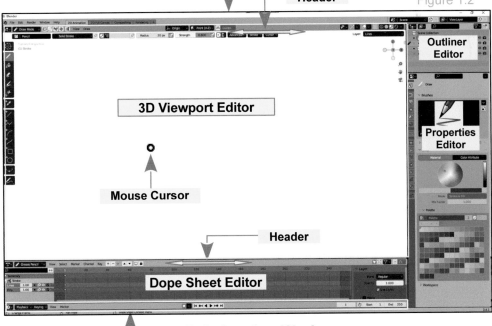

Figure 1.2

Header

Outliner Editor

3D Viewport Editor

Mouse Cursor

Properties Editor

Header

Dope Sheet Editor

Timeline Editor

2D Animation Workspace

The **2D Animation Workspace** comprizes five panels or windows which are called **Editors** in Blender. The Editors have a strip (usually at the top of the panel) called a **Header** containing buttons or sliders for activating functions or entering values. The big white panel taking up the majority of the Screen is the **3D Viewport Editor** where you draw and construct your **2D Animation**. The functions and values in the Headers affect what takes place in the Editor.

Yes! 2D Animation in the 3D Viewport Editor. The Grease Pencil is a 2D Environment within Blender 3D.

1.3 2D Animation

Traditionally **2D Animation** meant drawing a Character or Figure in a series of poses on separate sheets of paper then displaying each pose in quick succession creating the illusion of motion. The earliest method of achieving this was to simply flip the pages in a booklet. With the advent of photography the drawings were photographed creating slides which were combined into a film. When the film (movie) was played a very flickery image showed the character or figure moving; hence the expression, "Going to the Flicks."

This photographic process was developed and refined to the stage where full-length feature movies were produced and as you can imagine this involved creating thousands of slides. With computers and programs such as Blender this production procedure has been further developed and made available to anyone willing to undertake the learning curve. To discover how 2D Animation is accomplished using the Blender Grease Pencil work through the following, very basic, exercise.

1.4 Drawing a Stroke

With the **Mouse Cursor** in the **3D Viewport**, click LMB, hold and drag, release LMB to draw a **Stroke**.

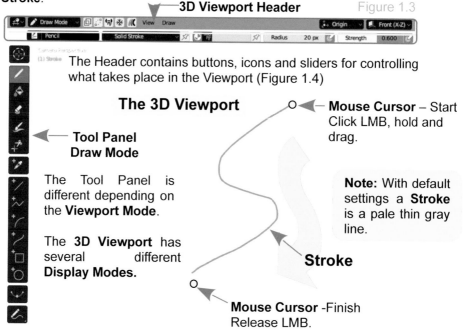

3D Viewport Header

Figure 1.3

The Header contains buttons, icons and sliders for controlling what takes place in the Viewport (Figure 1.4)

The 3D Viewport

Mouse Cursor – Start Click LMB, hold and drag.

Tool Panel
Draw Mode

The Tool Panel is different depending on the **Viewport Mode**.

The **3D Viewport** has several different **Display Modes**.

Note: With default settings a **Stroke** is a pale thin gray line.

Stroke

Mouse Cursor -Finish Release LMB.

Note the following: (Upper Left-Hand side of the 3D Viewport)

3D Viewport Editor (Button)

Figure 1.4

Draw Mode (Button – The Viewport has several different Modes)

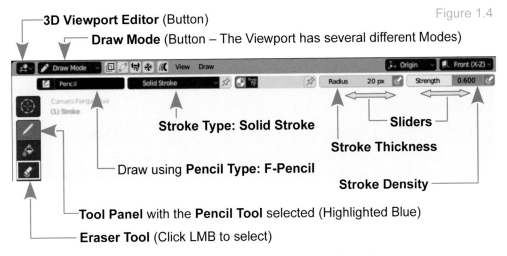

Stroke Type: Solid Stroke

Sliders

Stroke Thickness

Draw using **Pencil Type: F-Pencil**

Stroke Density

Tool Panel with the **Pencil Tool** selected (Highlighted Blue)

Eraser Tool (Click LMB to select)

Clicking (LMB) on a **Button** displays a selection menu with options.

> The default options mean you are working in **Draw Mode** using **Brush Type: F Pencil** with a **Solid Stroke.**

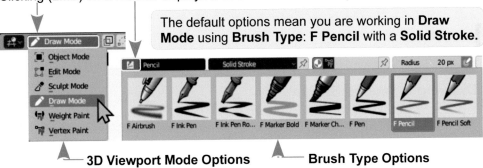

3D Viewport Mode Options   **Brush Type Options**

Where you see **Slider**, click in the panel, hold and drag left or right to alter the value.
Note: Radius is the thickness of the Stroke. **Strength** is the density of the Stroke.

Figure 1.5

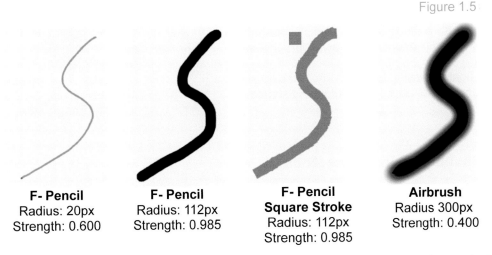

F- Pencil
Radius: 20px
Strength: 0.600

F- Pencil
Radius: 112px
Strength: 0.985

F- Pencil
Square Stroke
Radius: 112px
Strength: 0.985

Airbrush
Radius 300px
Strength: 0.400

Figure 1.5 demonstrates different **Stroke Draw** combinations which may be made. You will have to experiment with the different Stroke Types to become conversant with the full range. At this point the samples merely make you aware of what can be achieved.

1.5 Deleting - Undoing

When you perform an action, such as drawing a Stroke, it's a good idea to know how to make corrections, if a mistake is made.

Method One: Press **Ctrl + Z Key** on the Keyboard to **undo the last operation**. This will delete the last Stroke drawn. Repeatedly pressing Ctrl + Z removes previous successive operations.

Method Two: Select the **Eraser Tool** in the Tool Panel. The Mouse Cursor becomes a circle.

Figure 1.6a

Figure 1.6b

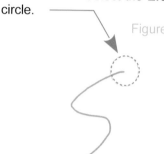

Position the circle over the Stroke, click, hold and drag to erase part of the Stroke.

1.6 Drawing a Second Stroke

With the Stroke drawn as shown in Figure 1.3 draw a second Stroke in the form of a circle (Figure 1.7).

At this point you are asked to use **your imagination** since this two-stroke Object will be animated.

As a suggestion consider the Object to be a balloon with a string attached which has been released and is about to float away into the sky.

As it floats away it sways in the breeze and appears smaller as it moves into the distance.

Second Stroke

Figure 1.7

First Stroke

Figure 1.3

Your Imagination

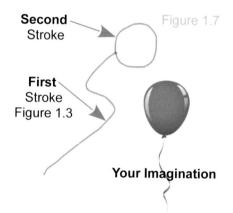

1.7 Positioning in Object Mode

The balloon consisting of two Strokes will be a **Character** in the Animation. The Character has been drawn with the 3D Viewport in **Draw Mode**. Remember, the white panel in the Screen, 2D Workspace is called the 3D Viewport.

The Character may not be positioned correctly to suit the intended Animation. To reposition the Character (the two Strokes) change the 3D Viewport Editor from Draw Mode to **Object Mode** (Figure 1.8). **Note:** The Tool Panel at the left of the Editor changes.

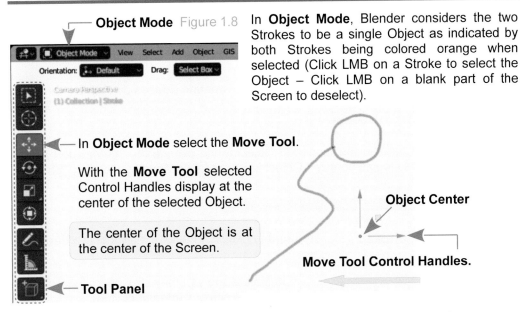

Object Mode Figure 1.8

In **Object Mode** select the **Move Tool**.

With the **Move Tool** selected Control Handles display at the center of the selected Object.

The center of the Object is at the center of the Screen.

Tool Panel

Object Center

Move Tool Control Handles.

In **Object Mode**, Blender considers the two Strokes to be a single Object as indicated by both Strokes being colored orange when selected (Click LMB on a Stroke to select the Object – Click LMB on a blank part of the Screen to deselect).

Click on a the red **Control Handle**, hold the Mouse button and drag horizontally. Click the blue Handle to move vertically.

Assuming you wish the balloon to float from left to right in the scene (see Figure 1.13) as it moves away into the background, position the Strokes towards the left of the Screen. Click on the Move Tool red Control Handle, hold and drag to the left.

With the balloon positioned this will be the **Start Position** for the Animation.

Animations are visualized and controlled in **Dope Sheet** and **Timeline Editors** which are the two panels at the bottom of the Screen (Figure 1.9).

1.8 Dope Sheet and Timeline

Dope Sheet Editor

Figure 1.9

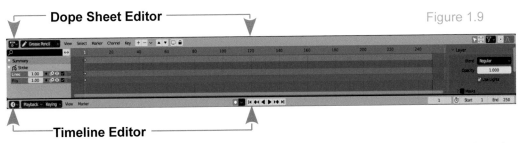

Timeline Editor

Each Editor Panel in Blender has an Icon representing the Editor Type. The icon is usually in the upper left-hand corner of the Editor (Figure 1.9). Clicking on any of these Icons displays the Editor selection Menu (Figure 1.10).

Figure 1.10

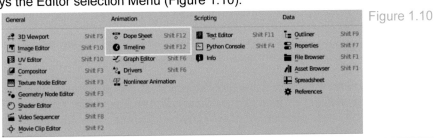

Blender may be customized to suit your personal preferences. By clicking the Editor Icon and selecting a different Editor Type in the menu changes the current Editor to the Type selected.

Have the **3D Viewport**, the **Dope Sheet** and the **Timeline Editors** displayed.

1.9 Manipulating Strokes

With the balloon Character positioned in Object Mode change the 3D Viewport to **Edit Mode**. **Tip:** You may toggle between Object Mode and Edit Mode by pressing **Tab**.

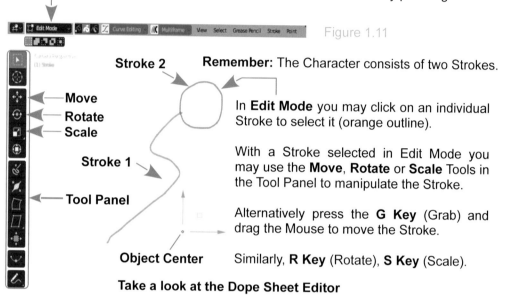

Figure 1.11

Stroke 2

Remember: The Character consists of two Strokes.

Move
Rotate
Scale

In **Edit Mode** you may click on an individual Stroke to select it (orange outline).

Stroke 1

With a Stroke selected in Edit Mode you may use the **Move**, **Rotate** or **Scale** Tools in the Tool Panel to manipulate the Stroke.

Tool Panel

Alternatively press the **G Key** (Grab) and drag the Mouse to move the Stroke.

Object Center

Similarly, **R Key** (Rotate), **S Key** (Scale).

Take a look at the Dope Sheet Editor

1.10 The Dope Sheet Editor

The horizontal graph in the **Dope Sheet Editor** represents the length of your Animation. By default the length is 250 Frames.

Figure 1.12   **Frame 250**

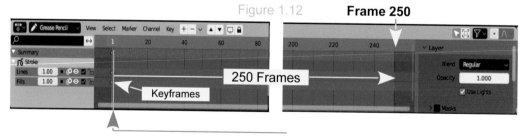

250 Frames

Keyframes

The vertical blue line at Frame 1 is the **Timeline Cursor**. You click on the blue rectangle at the top of the Cursor, hold and drag to position the Cursor in the Timeline.

Note the little yellow triangles at Frame 1 (the triangles will display white until you click to select them). The triangles represent **Keyframes** (Key Frames).

The principal of Animation in Computer Graphics is: The position and shape of Strokes is recorded at a specific Frame (a Keyframe) in the Animation Timeline. The Frame is determined by the position of the Timeline Cursor. The Strokes are manipulated and repositioned then a second Keyframe is set which records the status of the Strokes at the new Frame. The computer works out the status of the Strokes at all frames between the Keyframes. When the Animation is played you see each Frame in quick succession and are tricked into seeing the Character move.

1.11 Posing the Character

When you manipulate Strokes you are **Posing the Character**. You create a different **Pose** at each Keyframe in the Animation Timeline.

With the **3D Viewport in Edit Mode** move the Timeline Cursor to Frame 60 in the Animation Timeline. **Select the circle Stroke** (balloon), press the G Key (Grab) and drag the Mouse to reposition the circle. Press the S Key and drag the Mouse to Scale the balloon making it smaller (Figure 1.13).

Select the string Stroke. G Key drag - S Key scale - R Key rotate to reattach the string to the balloon.

Move the Timeline Cursor to frame 120 and repeat the operation moving the balloon and string further into the distance.

At each repositioning operation a Keyframe is inserted in the Timeline recording the Location, Rotation and Scale of the Strokes. You will also see a faint outline showing the preceding status of the Stroke. This is called **Onion Skinning** which is a reference aid for determining the relative position of Strokes.

In the **Timeline Editor** click the Jump to **Endpoint** button to return the Cursor to Frame One.

Figure 1.13

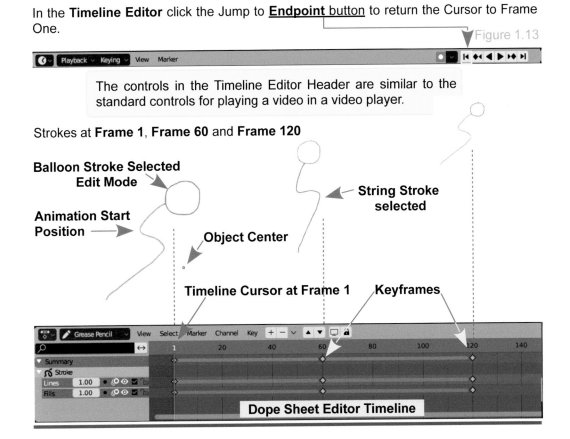

The controls in the Timeline Editor Header are similar to the standard controls for playing a video in a video player.

Strokes at **Frame 1**, **Frame 60** and **Frame 120**

Balloon Stroke Selected Edit Mode

String Stroke selected

Animation Start Position

Object Center

Timeline Cursor at Frame 1   **Keyframes**

Dope Sheet Editor Timeline

1.12 Playing the Animation

At this point you can play the Animation by pressing the **Play (forward) button** in the **Timeline Editor.**

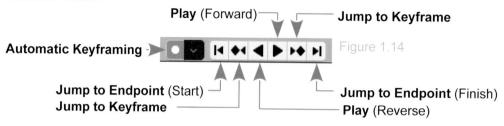

Play (Forward) ── Jump to Keyframe

Automatic Keyframing ──

Jump to Endpoint (Start) ── Jump to Endpoint (Finish)
Jump to Keyframe ── Play (Reverse)

1.13 Automatic Keyframing

When creating the Animation in the Dope Sheet Timeline, Keyframes have been automatically inserted at each location of the Timeline Cursor when a Stroke is repositioned. This occurs since **Automatic Keyframing** is activated in the Timeline Editor. You may disable this function by clicking on the Automatic Keyframe button. You manually enter Keyframes by, locating the Timeline Cursor, posing a Stroke then pressing the **I Key** on the Keyboard and selecting **Insert Blank Keyframe** in the menu that displays.

Note: Playing the Animation at this point will see the Strokes jump from the Pose at Frame 1 to Frame 60 to Frame 120 as the Timeline Cursor traverses the Timeline.

1.14 Interpolation

To smooth the Animation you employ the **Interpolation Function** to generate Frames between the Keyframes. Locate the Timeline Cursor between Frame 1 and frame 60.

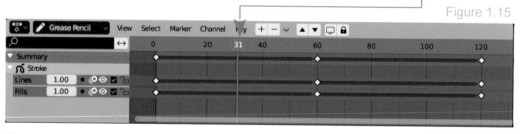

Have the **3D Viewport in Edit Mode.** In the 3D Viewport Header click on **Grease Pencil** and select **Interpolation Sequence** in the menu that displays.

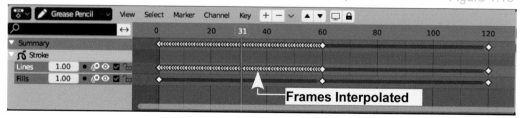

Frames Interpolated

Relocate the Timeline Cursor between Frame 60 and Frame 120 and repeat the procedure. Playing the Animation will see the balloon smoothly float across the Scene. You may view the Animation in Edit Mode or Object Mode.

1.15 Summary

The foregoing is a brief introduction which produces a rather crude Animation. In the following chapters you will be shown how to use Grease Pencil Tools and Techniques to refine the Animation adding color and background scenery and finally Render the Animation to a Video File.

Figure 1.17

1.16 To Continue

The essence of 2D Animation using the Grease Pencil is knowing how to construct characters and scenery by drawing Strokes. So far, a Stroke has been demonstrated as simply a line which may be manipulated and repositioned. A Stroke, however, is more than a line. By understanding how a Stroke is constructed and how it may be edited after it is drawn will enable you to control the detail in animation. It will also assist if you understand that drawing a 2D Stroke in the Viewport, is in fact, drawing in a 3D Environment.

All will be revealed as you progress through the following chapters but before moving on be aware of the surface you are drawing on when you draw a Stroke and the controls that are available for drawing.

1.17 The 3D Viewport Editor

The **3D Viewport** is configured inside Blenders 3D Architecture.

Figure 1.18

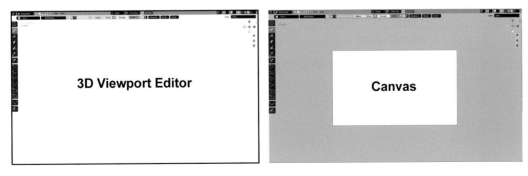

When you draw a Stroke in the 3D Viewport Editor you are drawing on a **Canvas**.

With the Mouse Cursor in the 3D Viewport Editor, scrolling the MMB out reveals the 2D Animation Canvas (Drawing Area - Figure 1.18).

Clicking MMB displays the Camera (Figure 1.19 L) which is a graphical representation of a Camera positioned in the 3D Environment to capture what is drawn on the Canvas.

Figure 1.19

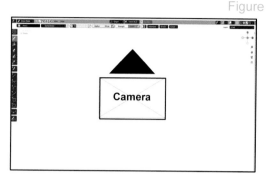
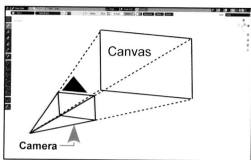

By clicking, holding and dragging MMB to the left and scrolling out again, shows the Camera pointing to the right. A representation of the Canvas has been sketched in the Viewport to demonstrate how the Camera sees the Canvas in the 3D Environment (Figure 1.19 R).

The Camera is positioned square on to the Canvas such that it captures the whole Canvas area which fills the entirety of the 3D Viewport Editor. When an Animation is created on the Canvas the Camera captures each Frame of the Animation as it is played.

Be aware that the Canvas can have multiple **Layers** on which you draw and that you may have multiple Canvases in a Scene. This will be explained in detail later in the book. For the time being revisit the **3D Viewport Editor** (Figure 1.4) and continue.

1.18 Editor Controls - Buttons, Icons and Sliders

Figure 1.20

Button: Click to display the **Editor Type selection Menu** (inset).

2D Animation Workspace   **Alternative Workspaces**

The **3D Viewport Editor in the 2D Animation Workspace** is one of a selection of Editors available.

An Editor may be changed to a different Editor Type by selecting from the selection menu.

Editor Type Selection Menu

Click the Button in the Header to display the menu.

To demonstrate changing Editor Types, click the Button in the Header and click on **Preferences** in the selection menu. The 3D Viewport Editor changes to the **Preferences Editor.**

Figure 1.21

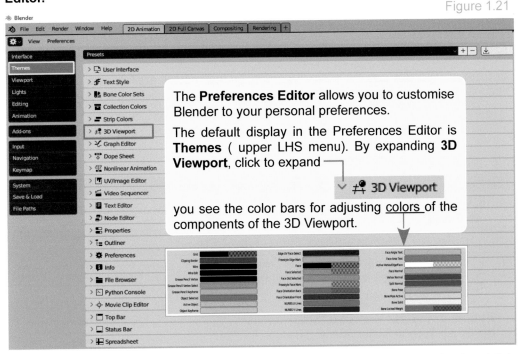

To change back to the **3D Viewport Editor** reopen the selection menu and select (click on) **3D Viewport**.

You will have occasion to change aspects of the 3D Viewport but for the time being examine the components of the default display. To begin, make the distinction between the **Blender Screen Header** and the **3D Viewport Header.**

Figure 1.22

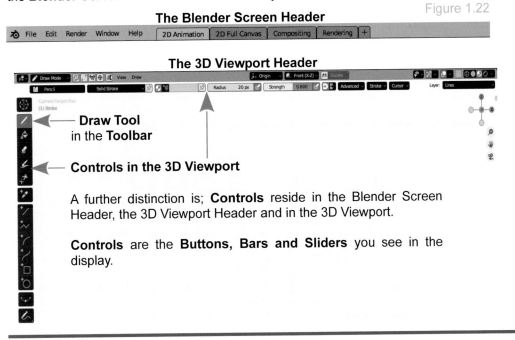

1.19 Editor Controls - Buttons, Bars, Icons and Sliders

Controls for the operation of the program are presented in the Headers and Panels in each Editor of the 2D Animation Workspace. The controls are in the form of Buttons, Sliders and Bars. Most Controls have an Icon (pictorial representation) of the function of the Control. The following examples define these terms.

Buttons in Blender can be a small square or rectangular area on the screen. Most buttons display with icons. A **Bar** is an elongated rectangle indicating a selection.

Button in the **3D Viewport Header** which opens the Editor selection menu. The **Icon** in the Button indicates that the current display is the 3D Viewport Editor.

The 3D Viewport Header

Figure 1.23

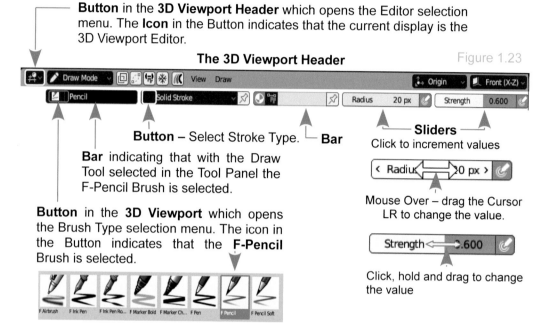

Button – Select Stroke Type. └─ **Bar**

Bar indicating that with the Draw Tool selected in the Tool Panel the F-Pencil Brush is selected.

Button in the **3D Viewport** which opens the Brush Type selection menu. The icon in the Button indicates that the **F-Pencil** Brush is selected.

Sliders — Click to increment values

Mouse Over – drag the Cursor LR to change the value.

Click, hold and drag to change the value

Sliders are elongated areas, usually containing a numeric value, which are modified by clicking, deleting and retyping the value, or clicking, holding and dragging the Mouse Cursor that displays on **Mouse Over**, left or right, to decrease or increase the value. Some sliders have a small arrow at either end which display when the Mouse Cursor is positioned over the Slider (Mouse Over). Click on an arrow to incrementally alter the value. Some sliders directly alter the display on the computer Screen.

For the Keyboard input, a command is: to press a specific Key or a series of Keys. Press **Shift + Ctrl + T Key** means, press and hold both the **Shift** and **Ctrl** Keys simultaneously and tap the **T Key** (Figure 1.24).

Figure 1.24

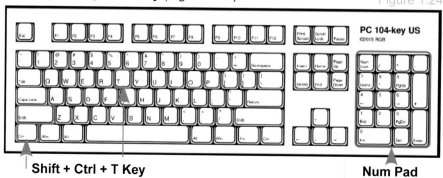

Shift + Ctrl + T Key   **Num Pad**

Num Pad (Number Pad) Keys are also used in which case the command is Press Num Pad 0 to 9 or Plus and Minus.

Controls in the Properties Editor

Besides the Controls in the 3D Viewport Headers there are Controls for affecting the 3D Viewport in the **Properties Editor**.

Properties Editor Figure 1.25

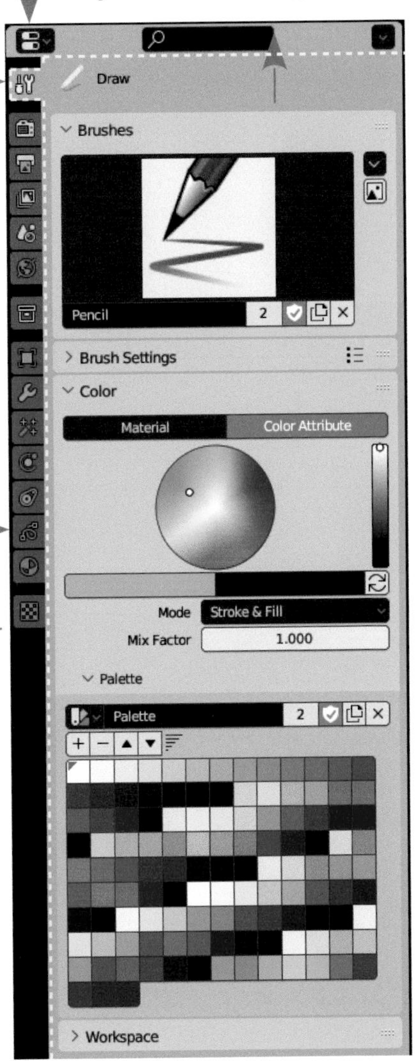

The Properties Editor (Lower RHS of Screen)

Active Tool and Workspace Properties

The **Properties Editor,** packs in a lot of options which at first glance are not obvious. Figure 1.25 shows the **Properties Editor** with the **Active Tool and Workspace Properties** displayed.

The vertical column of Tabs at the LHS of the Properties Editor select different panels for selecting different functions. By default the **Active Tool and Workspace Properties** panel is displayed. Mouse over on a button to see the panel display name. The Active Tool and Workspace controls are encapsulated by the broken yellow lines.

Figure 1.26

Object Data Properties

Object Data Properties

Panels containing controls may be hidden inside **Tabs**. In Figure 1.25 the **Color and Palette Tabs** are open displaying color selection options. The **Brush Settings Tab** is closed as is the Workspace Tab. To open a Tab click LMB on the **chevron** adjacent to the Tab name. To close a Tab click the chevron a second time.

Figure 1.27

Tab Open ⌄ Color

Tab Closed ⟩ Workspace

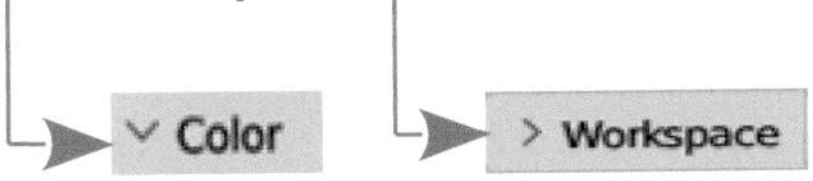

Note: The **Color Palette** is only operable when the Viewport Editor is in **Color Attribute Mode**. The default display is **Material Mode**.

To switch between Color Modes select the Mode in the **Properties Editor, Color Tab** or in the click the appropriate **Button in the 3D Viewport Header**.

Figure 1.28

Drawing Strokes

2.1 Drawing a Stroke

Drawing a Stroke (line) in the **2D Workspace** in the **3D Viewport** is as simple as clicking, holding and dragging the Mouse Cursor across the Screen. As demonstrated in the introduction (Chapter 1). The Stroke is Drawn according to the properties that have been set in the **3D Viewport Header**.

Be aware that a **Stroke may be Edited** once it has been drawn. Repositioning the Stroke, Scaling and Rotating were demonstrated in the introduction but there are more controls which allow Stroke configuration to suit what you are creating.

For the moment revisit drawing a Stroke in the **3D Viewport** with the default settings in the Header.

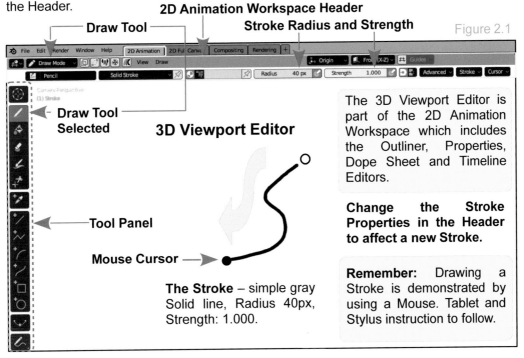

Figure 2.1

When you enter the **2D Animation Workspace**, by default, the **3D Viewport Editor** is in **Draw Mode** as seen in the **Viewport Editor Header**. Also, by default, the **Draw Tool** is selected (highlighted blue) in the Tool Panel and the Mouse Cursor displays as a small circle. The Mouse Cursor in the Viewport follows the Mouse movement.

Drawing Strokes will be described in terms of Drawing lines on the computer Screen using the Tools that are provided in the Grease Pencil Interface.

A **Stroke** is a Line which once Drawn may be Edited to refine its appearance or alter its shape. A Stroke (Line) is a component of a drawing. The component may be a Character or Object either of which may or may not be Animated in a Scene.

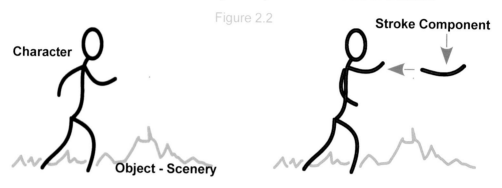

Figure 2.2

Character

Stroke Component

Object - Scenery

Figure 2.2 depicts a Character made up from a series of Stroke Components placed in a Scene. The Character is said to be Drawn in a Pose. The objective is to Animate the Character to walk in the Scene, therefore, the Character is Drawn in a Pose at a Frame in an Animation sequence. The Strokes comprising the Character are then Edited, in this case the arms are Rotated and repositioned (Translated) at another frame in the Animation sequence. When the Frames in the sequence are displayed in quick succession the Character will appear to move in the Scene.

To create this illusion Strokes are first Drawn then Edited. You may Draw Strokes freehand as shown in Figure 2.1 or use Grease Pencil Tools to generate Strokes (Figure 2.2). Similarly Tools are provided for Editing Strokes.

From humble beginnings depicted in the foregoing Figures fantastic results may be achieved as shown by **Grease Pencil Examples** at:

https://cloud.blender.org/p/gallery/

Figure 2.3

Example by: Nicholas Chamos

Example by: Sturmstudie & Lucern University

Example by: lien-ze ,Tsao

Example by: Kjartan Tysdal

2.2 Drawing on Layers

When you Draw a Stroke in the 3D Viewport you are Drawing on a **Layer**. The default 3D Viewport Editor in the 2D Animation Workspace has two Layers.

You see the Layers in the **Outliner Editor** at the top RHS of the Screen and in the **Layer Menu** in the upper RH corner of the 3D Viewport. One Layer is named **Lines** and the second Layer is named **Fills**.

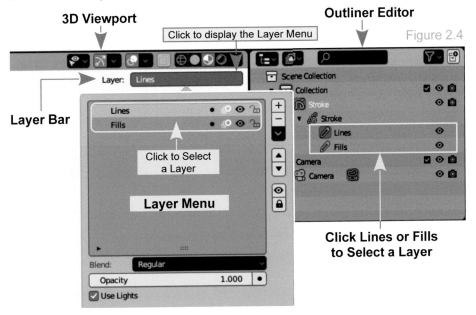

Figure 2.4

By default the Layer named Lines is selected (active) as seen in **Layer bar** in the 3D Viewport. To change Layers you display the **Layer Menu** then LMB click on either Lines or Fills in the menu. Alternatively you may click LMB on either Lines or Fills in the **Outliner Editor**.

Drawing Strokes on different Layers allows you to organize your work for complicated Scenes and for Animating. This is explained in Chapter 5 (The Canvas Explained).

For the time being be aware that Layers exist and that Strokes can be Drawn on different Layers and that you can add additional Layers in a Scene.

2.3 Editing Strokes

Figure 2.5

With the 3D Viewport in Edit Mode a Stroke may be Edited to alter its shape.

Examine the Stroke that has been drawn in Figure 2.1. **Note:** Radius 40px and Strength 1.000 set in the Header. In **Edit Mode** you will observe that the Stroke has a very faint line at its center.

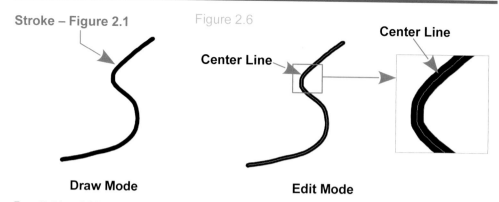

Stroke – Figure 2.1

Figure 2.6

Center Line

Center Line

Draw Mode　　　　　　　　**Edit Mode**

By clicking LMB on the Stroke it is selected as indicated by the center line being orange in color. Note: With a single Stroke drawn you may alternatively press the **A Key** to select the Stroke but if you have multiple Strokes drawn they will all be selected. In either case click LMB in an empty part of the Screen to deselect Strokes.

Note the Stroke selection Modes in the 3D Viewport Header.

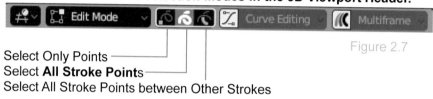

Figure 2.7

Select Only Points
Select **All Stroke Points**
Select All Stroke Points between Other Strokes

The default selection Mode is **All Stroke Points.**

By having **All Stroke Points** selected then clicking on the **Select Only Points** Mode you will see that the center of the Stroke is constructed with a **Series of Points**.

Point spacing depends on how you drag the Mouse.

Figure 2.8

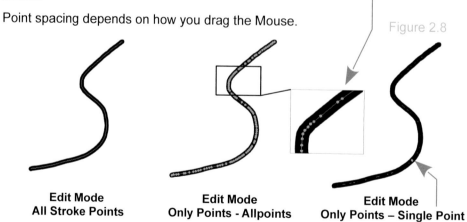

Edit Mode　　　　　**Edit Mode**　　　　　**Edit Mode**
All Stroke Points　　**Only Points - Allpoints**　**Only Points – Single Point**

Changing from All Stroke Points to Only Points displays all the Points making up the Stroke. By clicking LMB in the Screen, deselects All the Points and allows you to select a single Point.

Significance of Point Selection

Before realizing the significance of Point Selection consider the Point Selection in context with the Point Selection Option **Icons in the Header**.

Icons in the Header

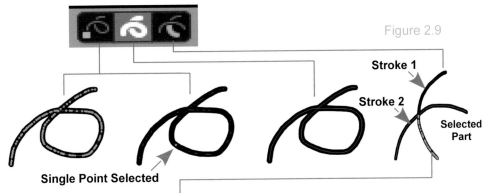

Figure 2.9

Stroke 1

Stroke 2

Selected Part

Single Point Selected

The **Select All Stroke Points between Other Strokes** option means, when there are two separate Strokes intersecting you may click LMB on part of a Stroke to select only that part.

OK, why Point Selection?

Figure 2.10

Select Only Points   (Be in Edit Mode)

Press the **C Key** to display the Selection Circle. Scroll MMB to adjust the Diameter of the Circle. Drag the Mouse to place the Circle over the Stroke and click LMB to select Points.

With Points selected press the R Key (Rotate), adjust the Circle of Influence that displays, drag the Mouse to Rotate the selectd Points.

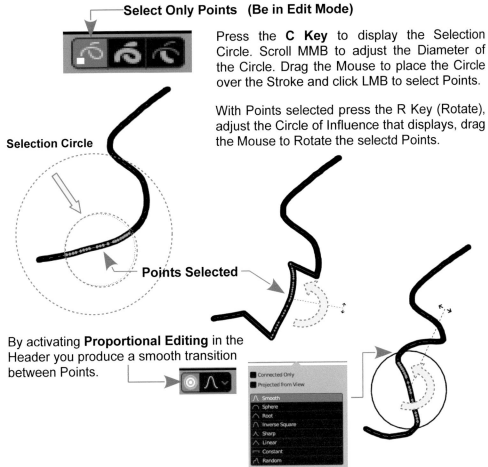

Selection Circle

Points Selected

By activating **Proportional Editing** in the Header you produce a smooth transition between Points.

Connected Only
Projected from View

Smooth
Sphere
Root
Inverse Square
Sharp
Linear
Constant
Random

Note: With Points selected you may press the **G Key** (Grab) and move Points or **S Key** (Scale) resize the selected group.

2.4 The Tool Panel

Section 2.3 has demonstrated that a Stroke may be Edited after it has been Drawn.

The quality of freehand drawing using the Mouse Cursor, with the Mouse or with a Drawing Stylus on a Tablet will depend on your drawing skill which will improve with practice. There are, however, tools available which allow you to produce professional effects. The Tools are found in the **Tool Panel** at the left-hand side of the **3D Viewport in Draw Mode**.

Figure 2.11

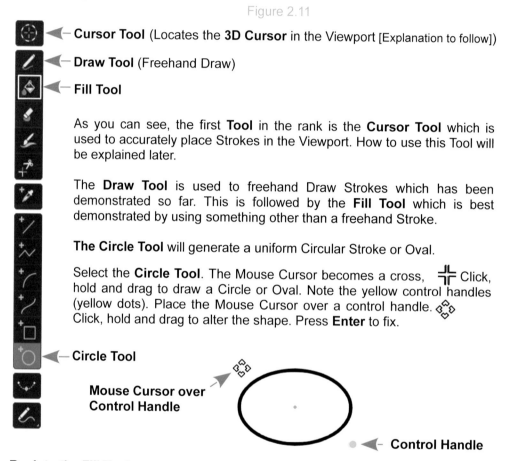

Cursor Tool (Locates the **3D Cursor** in the Viewport [Explanation to follow])

Draw Tool (Freehand Draw)

Fill Tool

As you can see, the first **Tool** in the rank is the **Cursor Tool** which is used to accurately place Strokes in the Viewport. How to use this Tool will be explained later.

The **Draw Tool** is used to freehand Draw Strokes which has been demonstrated so far. This is followed by the **Fill Tool** which is best demonstrated by using something other than a freehand Stroke.

The Circle Tool will generate a uniform Circular Stroke or Oval.

Select the **Circle Tool**. The Mouse Cursor becomes a cross, ⊥⊤ Click, hold and drag to draw a Circle or Oval. Note the yellow control handles (yellow dots). Place the Mouse Cursor over a control handle. Click, hold and drag to alter the shape. Press **Enter** to fix.

Circle Tool

Mouse Cursor over Control Handle

Control Handle

Back to the Fill Tool.

The Icon representing the Fill Tool suggests that the tool will act as a traditional **Bucket Fill** as used in many drawing applications. **NOT SO!** The Tool actually constructs a secondary stroke, mimicking the original, either inside or outside.

Note: The **Fill Tool** only works on the **Last Closed Stroke** selected in the 3D Viewport. Controls for the Fill Tool are located in the **Draw Mode, 3D Viewport Header**.

Figure 2.12

| Precision | 1.000 | Dilate/Contract | 1 px | Thickness | 5 px |

Fill Tool Controls

To use the Fill Tool, click on the icon in the Tool Panel. The Cursor in the 3D Viewport displays with a red circle. 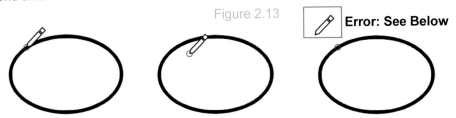 Drag the Cursor over the Stroke or inside the Stroke and click LMB. The Cursor displays with a Pen icon. Click LMB a second time.

Figure 2.13

Error: See Below

The Stroke is surrounded by a second Stroke either inside or outside the original depending on the settings in the Fill Tool Controls in the Header.

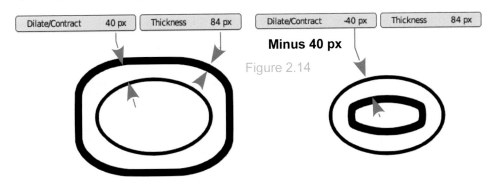

| Dilate/Contract | 40 px | | Thickness | 84 px |

Minus 40 px

Figure 2.14

| Dilate/Contract | -40 px | | Thickness | 84 px |

Note: If you place the **Pen Icon** outside the original Stroke an error message displays at the bottom of the Screen when attempting to generate the Fill.

Figure 2.15

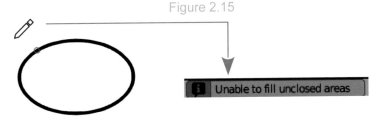

Unable to fill unclosed areas

The **Fill Tool** is perhaps one of the trickier Tools to use from the Tool Panel and has been demonstrated at this point as a prelude to discussing **Strokes, Lines and Fills**. The Fill Tool may, in fact, be used to Fill a Stroke with the right settings in the Header but there is another simpler way.

Figure 2.16

| Dilate/Contract | -40 px | | Thickness | 450 px |

Oval Stroke completely Filled with settings adjusted in the Header.

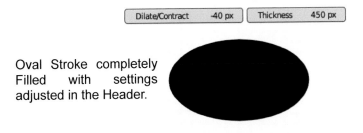

2.5 Strokes Lines and Fills

Figure 2.17

The Stroke Drawn in Figure 2.1 is said to be an **Open Stroke**.

This Stroke is also an **Open Stroke**

This Stroke is a **Closed Stroke**

Open

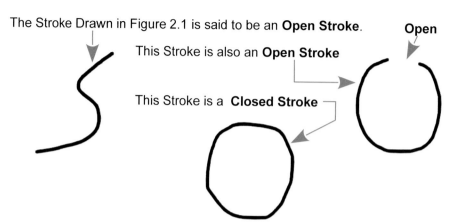

The Strokes Drawn above are all Drawn with a **Line only**. Strokes may be Drawn with a Line including a Fill or with only a Fill. The controls are located in the **Properties Editor, Material Properties, Surface Tab**.

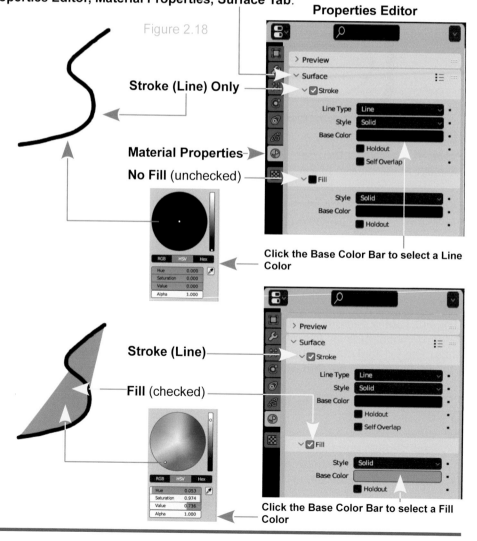

Properties Editor

Figure 2.18

Stroke (Line) Only

Material Properties

No Fill (unchecked)

Click the **Base Color Bar** to select a Line Color

Stroke (Line)

Fill (checked)

Click the **Base Color Bar** to select a Fill Color

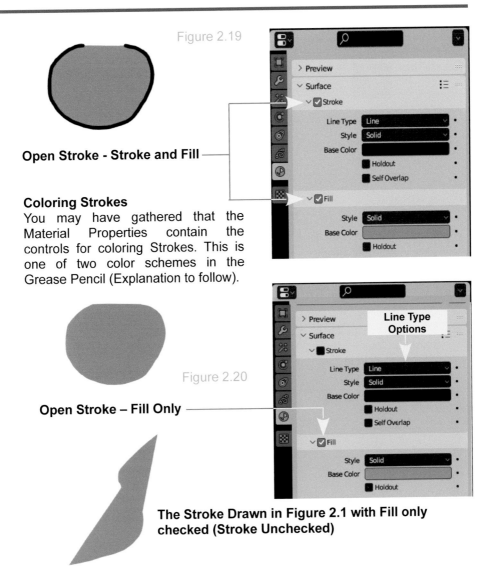

Figure 2.19

Open Stroke - Stroke and Fill

Coloring Strokes

You may have gathered that the Material Properties contain the controls for coloring Strokes. This is one of two color schemes in the Grease Pencil (Explanation to follow).

Figure 2.20

Open Stroke – Fill Only

Line Type Options

The Stroke Drawn in Figure 2.1 with Fill only checked (Stroke Unchecked)

Note: The **Line Type Options** in the **Surface Tab** for the Stroke.

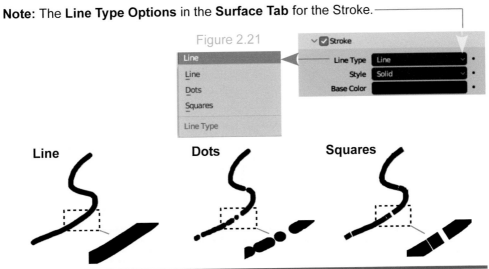

Figure 2.21

Line

Line

Dots

Squares

Line Type

Line   **Dots**   **Squares**

2.6 Draw Mode Tools

Erase Tool With the Erase Tool selected the Mouse Cursor becomes an Eraser Circle which you position over a Stroke, click, hold and drag to erase.

Figure 2.22

Tint Tool The **Tint Tool** allows you to change the color of part of a Stroke.

Settings in the Header

Figure 2.23

Click to display color selection.

Select a Color (click in the circle or select a swatch)

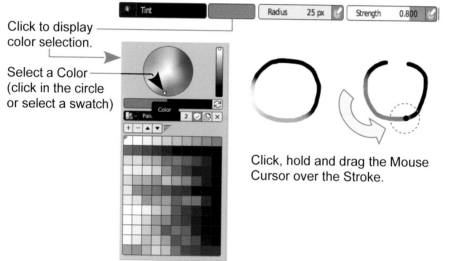

Click, hold and drag the Mouse Cursor over the Stroke.

Stroke Controls in the Header

Cutter Tool Cut or Trim part of a Stroke. The Mouse Cursor becomes a Knife Tool. Position the Knife, click, hold and drag a selection. Release the Mouse button.

Figure 2.24

Position the Cursor

Drag the Cursor to select part of the Stroke.

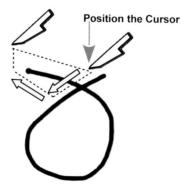 

Eyedropper The Eyedropper Tool allows you to select a color from a Stroke that has been previously drawn then draw a new stroke in the selected color.

The detail will be explained in conjunction with coloring Strokes to follow.

Figure 2.25

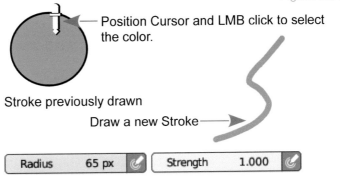

Position Cursor and LMB click to select the color.

Stroke previously drawn

Draw a new Stroke ———►

| Radius | 65 px | | Strength | 1.000 | |

Shape Tools

Line
Polyline
Arc
Curve
Box
Circle

Select a Tool. Click, hod and drag the Mouse Cursor in the 3D Viewport. Click on a **Control Handle,** drag and shape the Stroke. **Press Enter.**

Figure 2.26

With the **Polyline Tool**, click, hold drag – click, hold drag, to draw Stroke Segments.

Note: When using any of the Shape Tools a Taper may be applied to the Stroke. See Chapter 7 - 7.4.

Interpolate Tool The **Interpolate Tool** is used when Animating Strokes to create Frames between Keyframes (Explanation to follow).

Annotation Tool Click, hold and drag the Mouse Cursor to sketch diagrams or write notes on the Screen.

2.7 Brushes and Strokes

Up to this point Drawing Strokes has been demonstrated with the 3D Viewport in **Draw Mode** using the default settings in the Viewport Header. The exception being, the Radius has been increased to 40 px and the Strength has been increased to 1.000.

Click for Brush Options ┌─ **Click for Stroke Options**   Figure 2.27

When a Stroke is drawn with these settings it produces a simple black line on the Screen.

Figure 2.28

Note, however, the two other settings (values), **Pencil** and **Solid Stroke**. Pencil actually refers to the **Brush Type** - **F Pencil** which is one of eight **Brush Options** available.

Figure 2.29

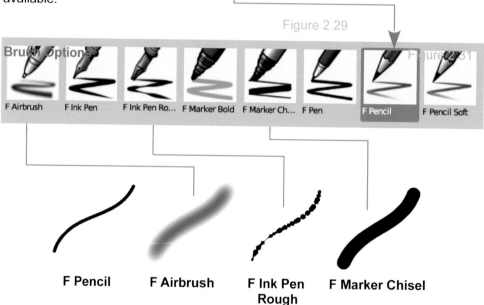

Different Brush options produce different Stroke (line) effects when drawn.

Stroke Options

Drawing a Line on the Screen has been referred to as Drawing a Stroke. A Stroke is actually a pre-configured Line Type or Style which may include characteristics such as the shape of the **line components** and color.

See the four **Stroke Options in the 3D Viewport, Draw Mode, Header** (Figure 2.30).

3D Viewport, Draw Mode, Header   Figure 2.30

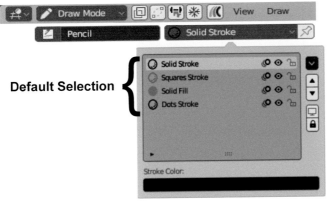

Default Selection

Note: The Stroke Types may be customized to your preference and Stroke Types can be added to the selection menu creating a Stroke Library.

Line Components

When a Stroke (line) is drawn it is constructed from a series of components (Dots).

Figure 2.31

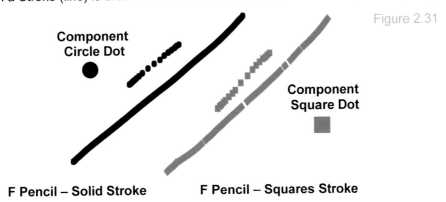

Component Circle Dot

Component Square Dot

F Pencil – Solid Stroke   **F Pencil – Squares Stroke**

Selecting the Stroke Option: **Dots Stroke** draws a line which displays the Circle Dot Component when the line is drawn. **Solid Stroke** is made up from the same Circle Dot but the Strokes are drawn close together producing the solid line.

Selecting Stroke Option: **Solid Fill** draws a **Fill without a Line**. (see Figure 2.20)

Stroke (line) drawn using the **Draw Mode – Curve Tool**.

The colored dots are the Control Handles for shaping the Curve which are displayed prior to pressing Enter on the Keyboard.

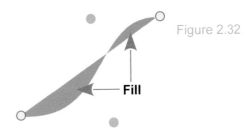

Figure 2.32

Fill

Customizing Stroke Types, Adding Stroke Types and Lines and Fills are best explained in conjunction with Coloring Strokes (Chapter 4 - 4.4).

3

Editing Strokes

3.1 Editing Strokes

When Strokes have been Drawn they may be Edited to refine their shape. They may be re-positioned, rotated and scaled and have special effects applied. Repositioning is performed with the 3D Viewport Editor in **Object Mode** and **Edit Mode**. Refining the shape of the Stroke is performed in **Sculpt Mode** and special effects are applied using the **Properties Editor, Special Effects Tabs**. There are also special **Grease Pencil Modifiers**. Modifiers are segments of code which create effects when applied to an Object or Stroke.

3.2 3D Viewport Modes

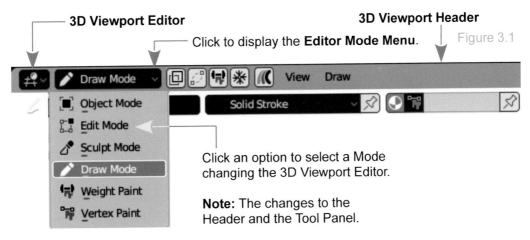

When the 2D Animation Workspace (Grease Pencil) is first opened the 3D Viewport is in **Draw Mode.**

Editing Strokes was briefly explained in Chapter 2 - 2.3 to make you aware that a Stroke could be modified once it had been drawn. It was demonstrated that a Stroke made up with a series of points which are control handles for manipulating the shape of the Stroke. The point selection was performed with the 3D Viewport in Edit Mode. Strokes may also be Edited in **Sculpt Mode**.

Note: Repositioning a Stroke in the Viewport is a form of Editing but how the repositioning is accomplished is best left until the **Canvas** is explained (Chapter 5).

3.3 Selecting Strokes for Editing

To Edit a Stroke you begin by selecting the Stroke in the 3D Viewport Editor. The basic selection procedure is to click LMB on a Stroke. How you select a Stroke depends on which 3D Viewport Mode you have opened.

Selecting in Object Mode

It will be construed that you can Edit Strokes in Object Mode since they may be Translated, Rotated and Scaled in the Viewport. Be aware, however, that you can not select individual Strokes in Object Mode.

Figure 3.2

With the two Strokes Drawn in Figure 3.2 in Draw Mode, when you change to Object Mode, both Strokes will be selected as indicated by their orange outlines. Clicking LMB in the Viewport will deselect the Strokes. Clicking LMB on one of the Strokes will select both Strokes. Performing a Translation, Rotation or Scale operation will affect both Strokes. This even applies when each Stroke is Drawn on a different Layer.

Selecting in Edit Mode

Changing from Draw Mode to Edit Mode shows the Strokes with a faint gray center line on each Stroke. Both Strokes are deselected. Click LMB on a Stroke to select. The center line displays orange.

Figure 3.3

S Stroke Selected

With the S Stroke selected (In Edit Mode) you may Translate, Rotate and Scale the Stroke relative to the O Stroke.

Figure 3.4

Transform Widget From the TransformTool

S stroke Translated, Rotated and Scaled

Note: Entering Edit Mode from Draw Mode with both Strokes deselected, pressing the **A Key** will select both (all) Strokes. Click LMB in the Viewport to deselect.

3.4 Editing in Object Mode

As previously shown, moving a Stroke in the 3D Viewport Editor is one type of Edit operation performed in **Object Mode**. You may also use the Rotate Tool and the Scale Tool or use the G (grab), R (rotate) or S (scale) Keys on the Keyboard. Performing these operations, is in effect, applying the function to the **Canvas.**

In Chapter 2 - 2.2 it was explained that **Strokes are Drawn on Layers**. In Object Mode all Strokes, in all Layers, will be affected. **You can not select individual Strokes when in Object Mode**. To Edit individual Strokes you have to be in **Edit Mode**.

An explanation of the Canvas and Layers will follow which will show why the expression, **in which Strokes are drawn**, instead of, **on which Strokes are drawn**, is used.

3.5 Editing in Edit Mode

To fully understand the Editing process, begin by recapping how the Stroke is constructed and viewed in the 3D Viewport Editor. Figure 3.5 shows a simple Stroke produced using the Draw Tool in Draw Mode. Default settings have been used in the Tool Header with the exception, the Radius has been increased to 50px and the Strength increased to 1.000 (**Note:** The examples are drawn using a Mouse).

Figure 3.5

Changing to **Object Mode**, the Stroke has an orange outline indicating that it is selected. You also see an orange dot at the center of the 3D Viewport Editor which is the center of the Canvas **in which the Stroke is Drawn**.

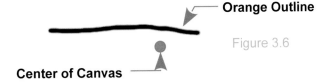

Orange Outline

Figure 3.6

Center of Canvas

You may click LMB anywhere in the 3D Viewport Editor to deselect the Stroke then LMB click on the Stroke again to re-select. When the Viewport Editor is placed in **Edit Mode** the stroke appears as it did in Draw Mode but with a very faint line along its center. You continue to see the center dot of the Canvas.

Figure 3.7

Click LMB on the center line to select the Stroke. The **center line displays orange**.

Figure 3.8

Center of Canvas

In **Edit Mode** there are the three **options** for displaying the selected Stroke.

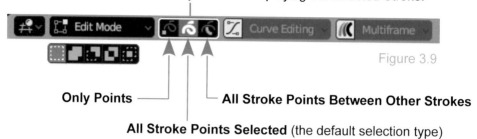

Figure 3.9

Only Points ── └── **All Stroke Points Between Other Strokes**

All Stroke Points Selected (the default selection type)

The significance of the selection options has been demonstrated in Chapter 2 - 2.3.

To recap the following is offered.

With a Stroke drawn Zoom in on the 3D Viewport Editor (scroll MMB) for a better view. Change the Viewport to **Only Points**, select Mode.

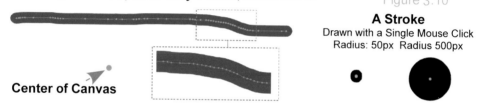

Figure 3.10

A Stroke
Drawn with a Single Mouse Click
Radius: 50px Radius 500px

Center of Canvas

As you see, the center line is made up from a series of small orange points connected together. The dots are **Control Points**. When they display orange they are selected, therefore, for this particular Stroke all the Control Points are selected. By clicking LMB in the Viewport Editor you deselect the points. Press the A Key to select all the points or Click LMB on a single point to select it or B Key and drag a rectangle (box select) or C Key (circle select) a series of points.

Figure 3.11

With points selected (in Edit Mode) they can be manipulated, editing the shape of the Stroke. To manipulate the points you can use the Move, Rotate and Scale Tools from the Tool Panel or press the G Key (Translate), R Key (Rotate) or S Key (Scale) on the Keyboard.

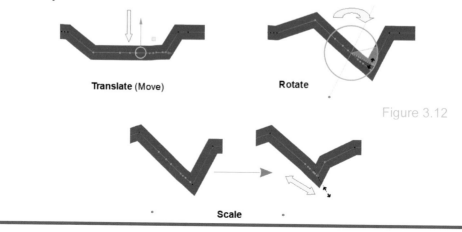

Translate (Move)   **Rotate**

Figure 3.12

Scale

3.6 Proportional Editing

Figure 3.13

In the preceding diagrams the manipulations produce sharp transitions in the shape of the Stroke. To produce smooth transitions, **Proportional Editing** is activated.

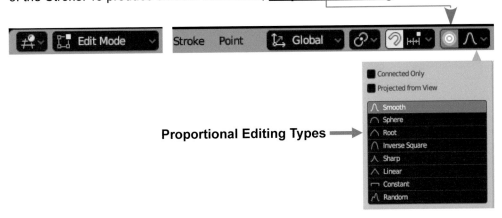

Proportional Editing Types

The following examples show Control Points in Edit Mode in relation to the settings in the Header prior to drawing in Draw Mode. The first two Strokes are drawn using the Draw Mode, Line Tool and the last Stroke is a freehand draw.

Figure 3.14

Control Points display with a Stroke selected in Edit Mode with Select Mode: Only Points

Note: Subdivisions

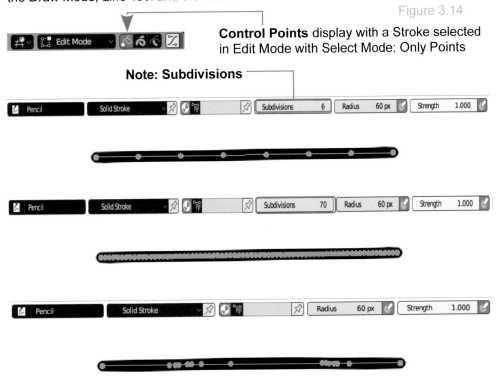

There is no Subdivision setting when freehand drawing. The number of Control Points created depends on how fast you draw the Stroke. This will usually be slow to start and slow at the finish. With any Stroke you can generate additional Control Points by selecting the Stroke (in Edit Mode), RMB click in the 3D Viewport and select **Subdivide** in the menu that displays. Repeat as many times as required.

With **Proportional Editing** activated and with **Smooth Falloff** selected, manipulations produce the following results.

In Edit Mode Press the B Key (Box Select) and drag a rectangle selecting Control Points. Press the G Key (Grab). Adjust the Circle of Influence (Scroll MMB) press the Z Key (Confines the translation to the Z Axis) and drag down.

Figure 3.15

First Stroke

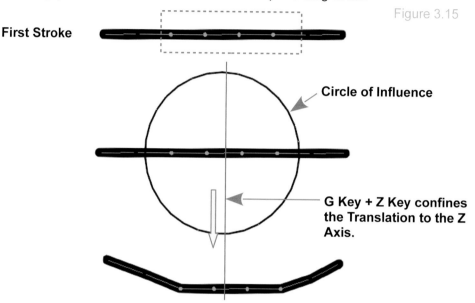

Circle of Influence

G Key + Z Key confines the Translation to the Z Axis.

Repeat the procedure with the Second Stroke to see the difference.

Second Stroke

Points Rotated (R Key Rotate)

Points Rotated and Scaled (R Key Rotate + S Key Scale)

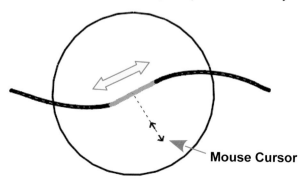

Mouse Cursor

3.7 Edit Mode Tools

As demonstrated, Editing a Stroke is manipulating Control Points to alter the shape of the Stroke or the position of the Stroke.

Remember: The purpose fore Editing a Stroke may be to draw a line creating a static display such as background scenery but Editing is also the primary method of posing a character for Animation.

With Strokes drawn there are several Tools available in the **Edit Mode Tool Panel** to assist. In Edit Mode have the Stroke Selected.

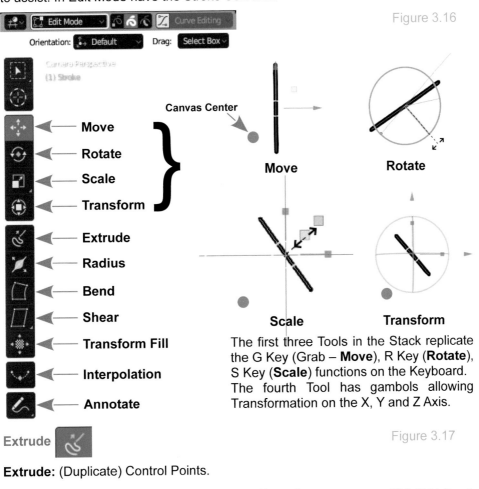

Figure 3.16

The first three Tools in the Stack replicate the G Key (Grab – **Move**), R Key (**Rotate**), S Key (**Scale**) functions on the Keyboard. The fourth Tool has gambols allowing Transformation on the X, Y and Z Axis.

Figure 3.17

Extrude: (Duplicate) Control Points.

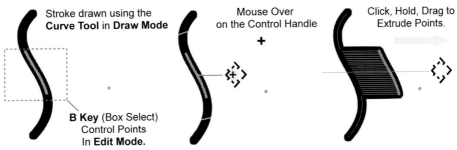

Radius: Expand or Contract the Radius of the Stroke associated with the selected Control Points. Stroke drawn using the Curve **Tool** in **Draw Mode.**

   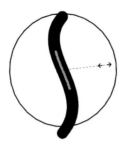 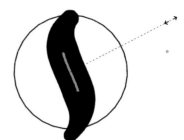

| Control Points
Selected
Edit Mode | With the Radius Tool
selected
Click LMB in the Viewport
Scroll MMB – Adjust Circle of
Influence | Drag the Mouse to alter the Radius
of the Strokes adjacent to the
selected Control Points |

Bend (Change the Shape) of a Curve adjacent to the selected Control Points relative to the Center of the Canvas. Stroke (Square) drawn using the Box Tool in Draw Mode.

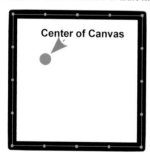 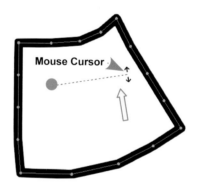

With the **Bend Tool** selected in **Edit Mode**, click LMB, hold and drag the Mouse bending the Curve relative to the Center of the Canvas.

Shear the Curve according to the Control Points selected.

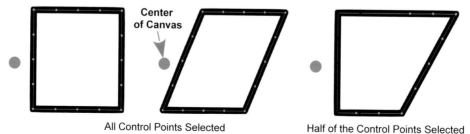

| All Control Points Selected | Half of the Control Points Selected |

The **Transform Fill** and **Interpolation** Tools will be left in abeyance at this time.

The **Annotation Tool** allows you to freehand sketch reference notes on the Screen.

3.8 Sculpt Mode Editing

Figure 3.21

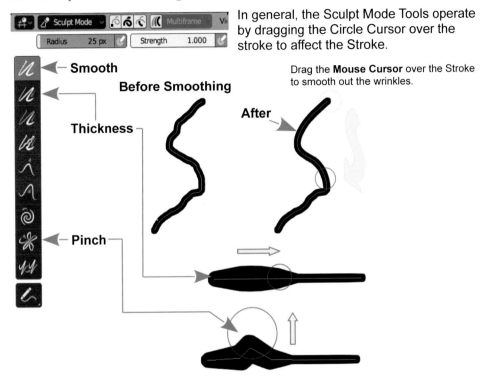

In general, the Sculpt Mode Tools operate by dragging the Circle Cursor over the stroke to affect the Stroke.

Drag the **Mouse Cursor** over the Stroke to smooth out the wrinkles.

3.9 Editing with Modifiers

Figure 3.22

Grease Pencil Modifiers are functions that affect how a Stroke appears and behaves. A Modifier is an in-built piece of code that you can apply to a Stroke. Modifiers are found in the **Properties Editor, Modifier Properties**.

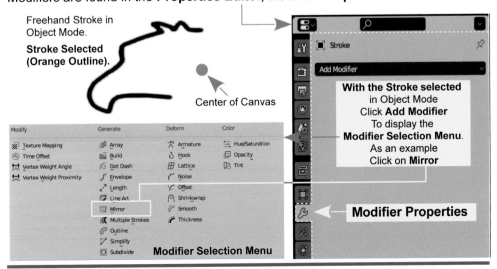

The **Mirror Modifier Panel** displays in the Properties Editor and the Stroke is Mirrored.

Figure 3.23

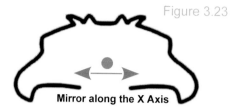

Mirror along the X Axis

Note: In the Mirror Modifier Panel, **Axis X** is highlighted blue. This is the Axis for the Mirror (Along the X Axis). You may alternatively select the Y or Z Axis.

Modifiers may be added to a Stroke in Draw Mode, Edit Mode or Object Mode.

With a Modifier added to a Stroke in a layer, the Modifier will affect all other Strokes that are subsequently drawn in the Layer.

> **Note:** Strokes drawn on the Canvas are drawn in Layers. There may be multiple Layers with different Strokes. (see Chapter 5).

To draw new Strokes without being affected by the Modifier you **Apply the Modifier** to the existing Strokes.

Figure 3.24

To cancel the effect of a Modifier, click **X**.

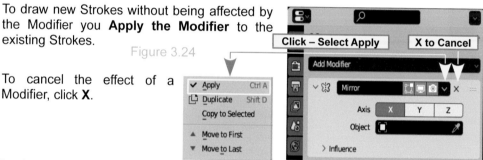

In the Modifier selection menu, generally speaking, the **Generate Category** of Modifiers is used to create Strokes. Experiment with the different types to be conversant with their effects. One of particular interest will be the **Build Modifier**.

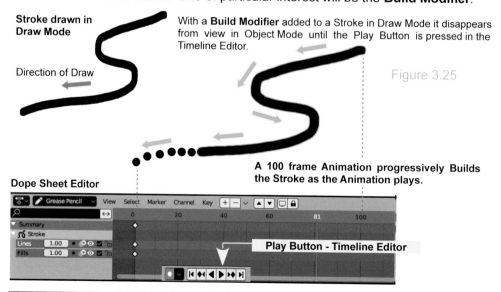

Stroke drawn in Draw Mode

Direction of Draw

With a **Build Modifier** added to a Stroke in Draw Mode it disappears from view in Object Mode until the Play Button is pressed in the Timeline Editor.

Figure 3.25

A 100 frame Animation progressively Builds the Stroke as the Animation plays.

Dope Sheet Editor

Play Button - Timeline Editor

3.10 Pre-Constructed Strokes

Blender provides two examples of preconstructed Strokes which you may use as a starting point. You may add these to a Scene then Edit them to suit your requirements.

With the **3D Viewport** in **Object Mode**, click **Add** in the Header, mouse over on **Grease Pencil** and select **Stroke** or **Monkey**.

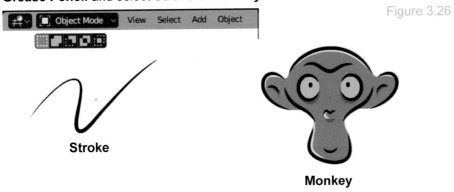

Figure 3.26

Stroke

Monkey

Blender has a pre-constructed 3D model of a Monkey affectionately named **Suzanne** which is used for demonstration purposes. Suzanne is also incorporated in the Grease Pencil in 2D.

As you see Suzanne is made up with a nice sunburned face, lighter colored eyes with highlights of the same color and black lines.

Suzanne will be used to help explain features of Stroke construction a little later but for now it is nice to know that she exists and where she lives. If you object to the Monkey being named Suzanne or being a she, just call her Bruce. She won't mind.

Figure 3.27

Suzanne with a rather clumsy Edit

Pre-constructed Strokes may be added to the selection menu and Strokes may be appended from a Blender file that you have saved. The how and why will be put in abeyance for the time being.

In the meantime Coloring and Customizing Strokes will be explained. Suzanne will help out in the explanation.

Keep in mind, drawing Strokes, colored or otherwise, is not to draw a picture but to create the components of a Character for Animation.

Coloring and Customizing Strokes / Brushes

Strokes have been demonstrated thus far, generally, employing a black color. In Chapter 2 – Section 2.5 Closed and Open Strokes were mentioned and shown in Figures 2.17 and 2.18 with a different color Stroke and a different color Fill.

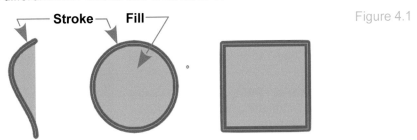

Stroke **Fill**

Figure 4.1

Drawing a Stroke with the default settings in the **3D Viewport Header** produces a black Stroke with **No Fill**.

Note: The default settings use the **F-Pencil** with **Solid Stroke**.

Figure 4.2

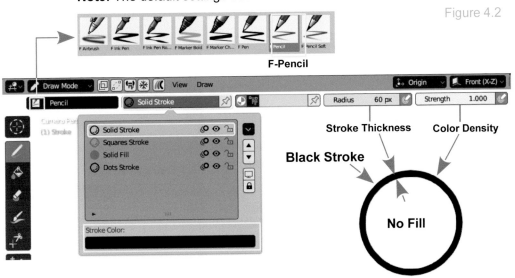

The Black color of the Stroke is being determined by values set in the **Properties Editor, Active Tool and Workspace Settings, Color Tab.**

4.1 Color Schemes

There are two **Color Schemes** in the Blender Grease Pencil which you select in the **3D Viewport Header** or in the **Properties Editor, Active Tool and Workspace Tab.**

The two Schemes are named **Material** and **Color Attribute.**

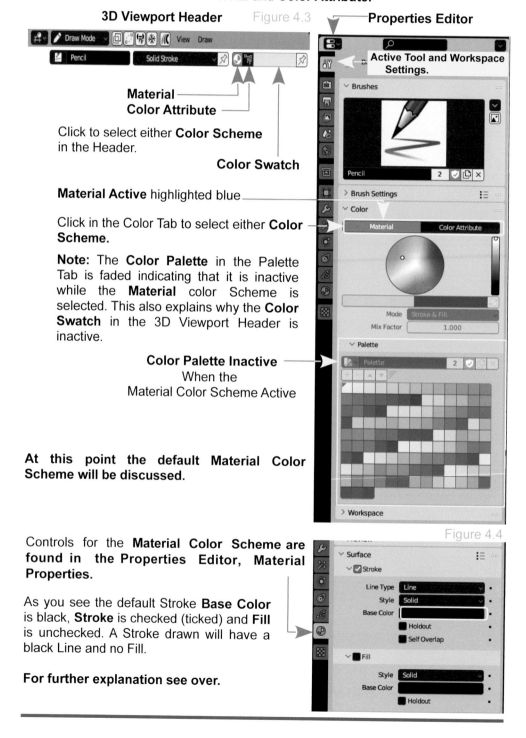

3D Viewport Header   Figure 4.3   **Properties Editor**

Material
Color Attribute

Click to select either **Color Scheme** in the Header.

Color Swatch

Material Active highlighted blue

Click in the Color Tab to select either **Color Scheme.**

Note: The **Color Palette** in the Palette Tab is faded indicating that it is inactive while the **Material** color Scheme is selected. This also explains why the **Color Swatch** in the 3D Viewport Header is inactive.

Color Palette Inactive
When the
Material Color Scheme Active

Active Tool and Workspace Settings.

At this point the default **Material Color Scheme will be discussed.**

Figure 4.4

Controls for the **Material Color Scheme are found in the Properties Editor, Material Properties.**

As you see the default Stroke **Base Color** is black, **Stroke** is checked (ticked) and **Fill** is unchecked. A Stroke drawn will have a black Line and no Fill.

For further explanation see over.

4.2 The Default Material Color Scheme

3D Viewport Header (LHS)   Figure 4.5   **Properties Editor**

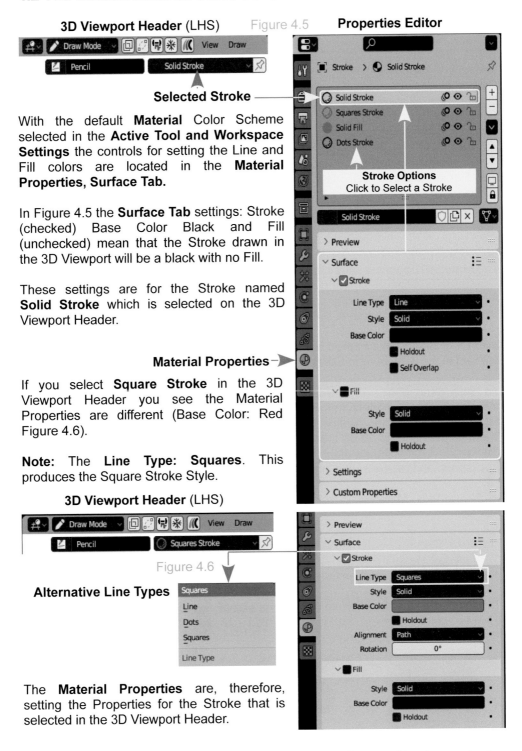

Selected Stroke

With the default **Material** Color Scheme selected in the **Active Tool and Workspace Settings** the controls for setting the Line and Fill colors are located in the **Material Properties, Surface Tab.**

In Figure 4.5 the **Surface Tab** settings: Stroke (checked) Base Color Black and Fill (unchecked) mean that the Stroke drawn in the 3D Viewport will be a black with no Fill.

These settings are for the Stroke named **Solid Stroke** which is selected on the 3D Viewport Header.

Material Properties→

If you select **Square Stroke** in the 3D Viewport Header you see the Material Properties are different (Base Color: Red Figure 4.6).

Note: The **Line Type: Squares**. This produces the Square Stroke Style.

3D Viewport Header (LHS)

Figure 4.6

Alternative Line Types

The **Material Properties** are, therefore, setting the Properties for the Stroke that is selected in the 3D Viewport Header.

The **Stroke Options** may be selected in the 3D Viewport Header or in the Properties Editor.

45

4.3 Adding New Strokes

The default Stroke Selection is: **Solid Stroke, Square Stroke, Solid Fill and Dots Stroke** which are arbitrary names for Strokes with different Properties. You may change the Properties for the default Strokes or you can create new Strokes and add to the Stroke Options list.

Figure 4.7

To create a new Stroke, have the **Properties Editor, Material Properties** open. At the RHS of the Stroke Options list, click on the **Cross button**.

Material Properties →

Properties Editor

Click the Cross

Click New

The Material Properties disappear except for a **New button**. Click on **New**.

Figure 4.8

A new Stroke is added to the Options list named **Material**. This is the name of the new Stroke.

Note: The new Stroke named **Material** has been entered in the 3D Viewport Editor Header.

You may rename the new Stroke to something meaningful to your project. In the Stroke Options list in the Properties Editor. Double click o **Material** (name turns black) then single click to display the Typing Cursor at the end of the name. Backspace and retype a new, press **Enter**.

In Figure 4.8 **Material** is renamed **My New Stroke.**

The new Stroke is automatically entered in the 3D Viewport Header and is ready to be used for drawing a Stroke in the Viewport.

The Properties for **New Stroke** are as you see in the Material Properties, Surface Tab. You can alter the setting to your requirements.

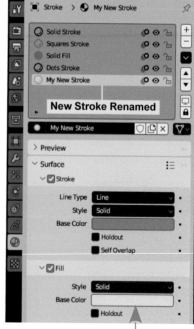

New Stroke Renamed

Click to select a Color

Color Brightness Slider

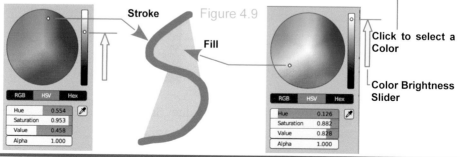

Stroke

Figure 4.9

Fill

4.4 Customizing Strokes

In the preceding examples, a New Stroke has been added to the Stroke Options List and new Material Properties (Color) have been assigned to the new Stroke.

Strokes may be customized (have properties assigned) which allow the drawing of something other than color. In this instance a PNG Image with a transparent background will be used as a Texture.

Figure 4.10

Figure 4.11

PNG Image File named
ScreenHunter 5333.png

To demonstrate a New Stroke Option will be created with **Stroke, Line Style, Texture**.

Create a New Stroke and name it **Texture Stroke.**

In the **Properties Editor, Material Properties, Surface Tab** have **Stroke** checked, with **Style: Texture.**

When **Texture** is selected the **Open button** displays. Click **Open** and navigate in Blender File View to where you have your Texture Image saved (See Chapter 18).

When you select the Texture Image the Material Properties will display the Image Name.

Drawing a Stroke in the 3D Viewport draws with the Texture (Figure 4.13).

Figure 4.12

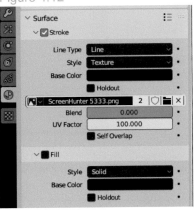

Figure 4.13

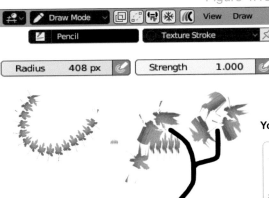

You may use any Image saved on your PC

4.5 The Color Attribute Color Scheme

Figure 4.14

The **Color Attribute**, Color Scheme, is activated by clicking Color Attribute in the Properties Editor, Active Tool and Workspace settings.

With Color Attribute active you are able to select colors in the Color Palette or from the Color Picker Circle in the Color Tab.

By default a pale green color is selected which is seen in Color tab and in the Draw Mode, 3D Viewport Header.

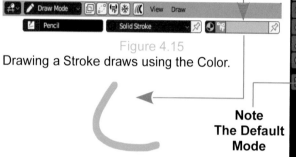

Figure 4.15

Drawing a Stroke draws using the Color.

Note
The Default
Mode

Whether a Stroke is drawn or a Fill is drawn depends on the selection in the **Material Properties.**

Figure 4.16

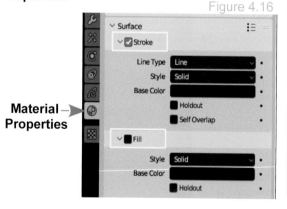

Material Properties

Remember: The Stroke / Fill and Color settings are for the particular Stroke selected in the Viewport Header.

Solid Stroke

Figure 4.17

Important: To draw Strokes with a selection using **Color Attributes** or similarly to draw Fills, you must have Strokes and or Fills checked in the Material Properties. This is despite the **Mode Options in the Properties Editor, Active Tool and Workspace Properties, Color Tab.**

The following will attempt to demonstrate.

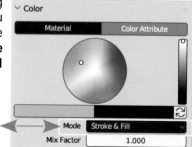

In the **Properties Editor, Material Properties** (Figure 4.16) have both **Stroke** and **Fill** checked.

In the **3D Viewport Editor Header**, with **Solid Stroke** selected, increase the **Radius** value to 100px and the **Strength** value to 1.000.

In the **Properties Editor, Active Tool and Workspace, Color Palette** select a bright red color. Note the default **Mode: Stroke & Fill** (Figure 4.17).

In the 3D Viewport, Draw Mode, draw a circle Stroke using the Circle Tool from the Tool Pane. Figure 4.18

The Circle drawn has a Red Stroke and a red Fill since you have Stroke and Fill checked in the Material Properties. The red color is applied to both the Stroke and Fill since Stroke & Fill is the Mode selected in Color Tab (Figure 4.17).

In the Color Tab change the **Mode** to **Stroke** and draw a second circle.

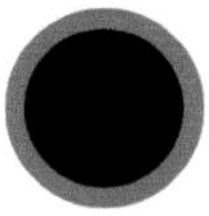

Figure 4.19

When drawing the second circle the Stroke uses the red color (you only have Mode: Stroke selected) and the Fill color reverts to the color selected in the Material Properties (black).

If you uncheck Fill in the Material Properties the Fill is not drawn.

Leave **Fill** checked in the **Material Properties** and change the Mode in the Color tab to **Fill** (Fill only). Figure 4.20

Drawing a third Stroke shows the Fill using the red color and the Stroke color reverting to the black that is set in the Material Properties.

4.6 Custom Colors

The interrelation between colors in the Material Properties and colors in the Color Attributes may be used to create custom colors.

Figure 4.21

Material Properties

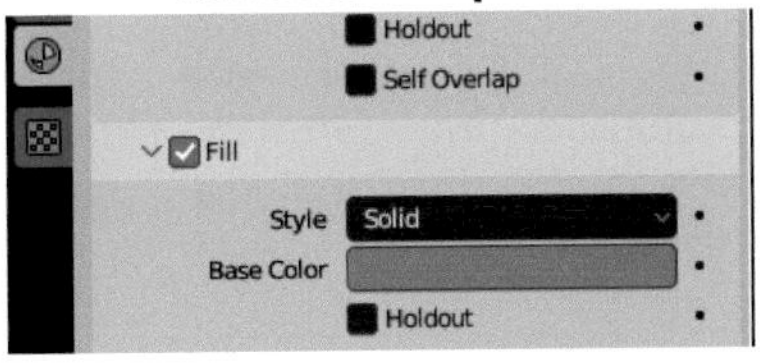

As an example have **Fill** only checked in the **Material Properties** with a bright Base Color selected. In the **Color Attributes** have **Mode: Fill** and select a different color.

Figure 4.22
Color Attributes

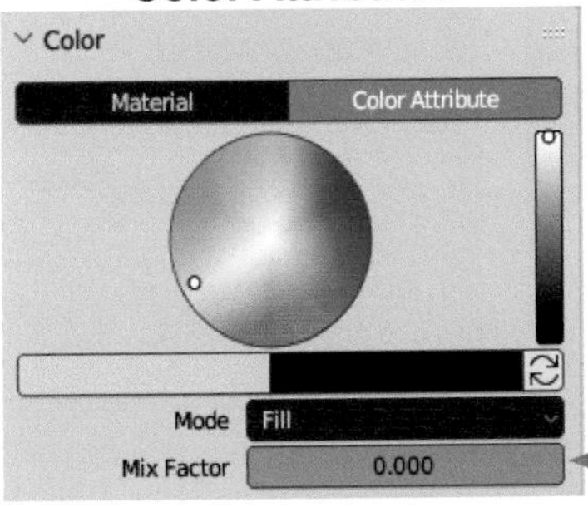

3D Viewport

Adjust the Mix Factor for Custom Colors
Circle Strokes in the 3D Viewport

← **Mix Factor**

Figure 4.23

The **Color Attribute Palette** has a good choice of Color Swatches but as you develop a Scene you will create new color combinations which you will want to reuse.

By clicking on the color bar below the Color Picker Circle you can display the RGB, HSV and Hex values for the selected color.

RGB, HSV and Hex values

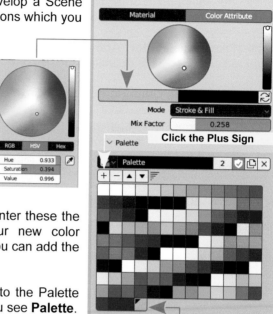

Click the Plus Sign

You could record the values and enter these the next time you wish to use your new color combination but for convenience you can add the combination to the Color Palette.

To add the color in the Color Bar to the Palette click the Plus **sign** below where you see **Palette**.

Click **Minus to delete**.

New Color Added

4.7 Color Workspace

Properties Editor—
Color Attribute

You will have observed that, when working with colors, you frequently have to switch the Properties Editor between the Material Properties display and the Color Attribute display.

Figure 4.24

Properties Editor—
Material Properties

For convenience you may configure the Grease Pencil Interface to include both displays.

The Blender Interface may be configured to your personal preference.

Editors may be added and arranged to suit a personal workflow creating a customized **Workspace**.

To create a **Color Workspace** mouse over on the corner of an Editor (Mouse Cursor displays as a cross). RMB click and select **Vertical Split** in the menu that displays.

Note: Dragging left splits the 3D Viewport, dragging right would split the Outliner Editor.

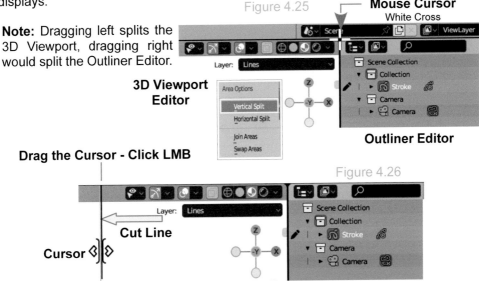

Figure 4.25

Mouse Cursor
White Cross

3D Viewport Editor

Outliner Editor

Drag the Cursor - Click LMB

Figure 4.26

Cut Line

Cursor

Click the Editor Icon and change the new window to the **Properties Editor**. Select the **Material Properties.**

Figure 4.27

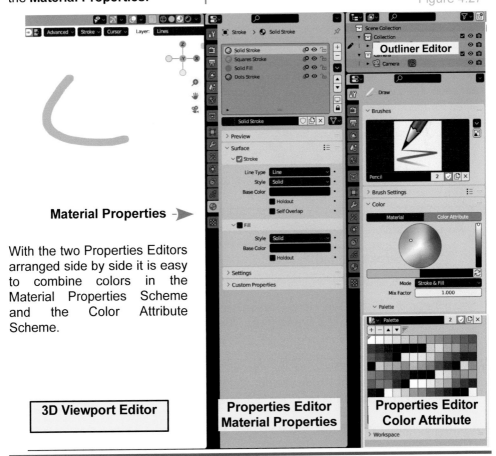

Material Properties ➤

With the two Properties Editors arranged side by side it is easy to combine colors in the Material Properties Scheme and the Color Attribute Scheme.

3D Viewport Editor

Properties Editor Material Properties

Properties Editor Color Attribute

4.8 Adding and Customizing Brushes

As you have seen new Strokes may be Customized and Added. Similarly, new **Brushes** may be created.

Before creating a new Brush be aware, that in some cases, a Stroke is **Pinned to the Brush**. This means when you select that particular Brush you can not change the associated **Stroke Type**. You can change the color but not the Stroke Type.

Brush Types

Figure 4.28

Figure 4.29

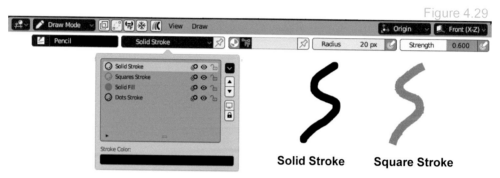

Solid Stroke   **Square Stroke**

The default Brush Type is the **F-Pencil**. The default Stroke Type associated with the F-Pencil Brush is **Solid Stroke**. You may select any of the Stroke Types in the selection menu to associate with the Brush, thus employing the Stroke color that has been set for that Stroke Type. You may also adjust the Radius and Strength values for the Stroke.

Brush Types

Figure 4.30

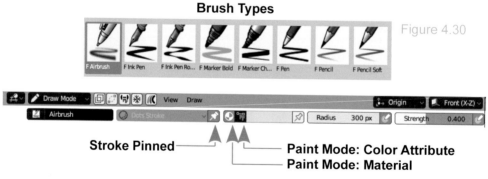

Stroke Pinned ────┘   └─── **Paint Mode: Color Attribute**
                                    └─── **Paint Mode: Material**

If you change the Brush Type to **F - Airbrush** you are unable to access the Stroke selection menu to change the Stroke Type. Stroke Type: **Dots Stroke** is **Pinned** to the Airbrush.

You can change the Stroke Color by selecting **Paint Mode: Material** (the Stroke base Color in the Material Properties) or **Paint Mode: Color Attribute** (the Stroke Color selected in Color Attribute, Color Scheme).

With this knowledge you can create a new Brush Type.

Properties Editor

The **Brush Type** selection menu accessed in the 3D Viewport, Draw Mode Header is replicated in the **Properties Editor, Active Tool and Workspace Properties** **Brushes Tab.**

Figure 4.31

Click LMB to display

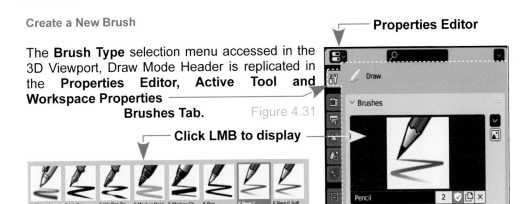

To create a new Brush click the **Add Drawing Brush button.**

A new Brush is created named **Pencil.001**. Click in the name bar and retype a new name suitable for your application (Maple Leaf).

Figure 4.32

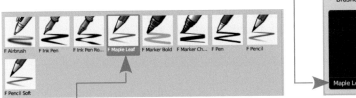

The **new Brush Type** is added to the selection menu.

At this stage the new Brush, **F Maple Leaf,** is associated with the Stroke named **Solid Stroke** and when used to draw in the 3D Viewport will draw a Stroke in accordance with the settings for Solid Stroke.

Figure 4.33

In this demonstration the new Brush will be set to draw using the Maple Leaf image employed in Section 4.4. To change the icon in the selection menu to represent the Maple Leaf click the **Custom Icon button** in the **Properties Editor, Brushes Tab**.

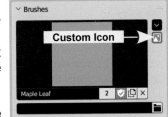

Custom Icon

Click the **Accept button**, navigate to your image file and click **Accept**. The image displays as the Icon for the new Brush.

Figure 4.34

Note: Displaying the image as the Icon for the Brush **does NOT** set the Brush to draw using the image.

Accept Button

To have the new Brush draw, using the image, create a Customized Stroke as described in Section 4.4. In the 3D Viewport Header, <u>**Pin the Stroke to th**</u> <u>**Brush**</u>.

Figure 4.35

Draw Mode — View Draw — Origin — Front (X-Z)

Maple Leaf — Solid Stroke — Radius — 300 px — Strength — 1.000

Set the Radius and Strength values for the Stroke.

With the new Stroke selected in the 3D Viewport Header you can draw Maple Leaf Strokes in the Viewport.

Figure 4.36

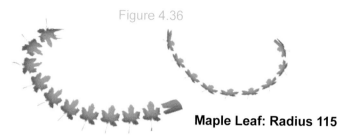

Maple Leaf: Radius 115

Maple Leaf: Radius 300

Adjust the Radius and Strength values to suit.

4.9 Downloading and Appending Brushes

An alternative to creating your own New Brushes is to download a Brush Pack from the internet. One source is: **Pepland_brush_pack_V1.zip**. Go to:

https://cloud.blender.org/p/gallery/5ccfe64353b85e279cf72acd

At this address, scroll down to find a video tutorial describing how to Import Brushes into the Grease Pencil for Blender 2.8 (Beta). Below the video tutorial is a Download link. The download gets you the **Pepland_brush_pack_V1 only for Blender 2.zip** file.

At this point, if you are unfamiliar with Navigating and Saving in Blender see Chapter 18.

It is best to create a new Folder on your PC for this exercise. For example create a Folder named **Brush_Pack** on your C: Drive.

Unzip the downloaded ZIP file using WinRar or 7-Zip to the folder. The unzipped file produces **pepland_GP_brush_pack_V1.blend** which is a Blender file.

Be aware that Elements from one Blender file may be Appended into another Blender file.

In Blender with the **2D Animation Grease Pencil** opened, click **File** in the **Screen Header** and select **Save As** in the menu that displays. Navigate to the Brush_Pack Folder, give the file a new name (**Brush_Pack.blend**) and click **Save As**. This gives you a copy of the default Grease Pencil start-up file in which to work.

The objective is to **Add Brushes** (Append) from the **pepland_GP_brush_Pack_V1.blend** file into the newly created copy of the default Blender File (Brush_Pack.blend).

You may Append the Brushes into any Blender file you are working on giving you, in effect, a Library of Brush Types.

To summarize: At this point you have a Folder on your C: Drive named Brush_Pack containing two Files (the unzipped pepland blender file and the Brush_Pack.blend file you have just saved).

With the new Brush_Pack.blend file opened. ⚙ Blender [C:\Brush_Pack\Brush_Pack.blend]

With this new file open click **File** in the Screen Header followed by **Append**.

Blender File View opens where you navigate to the Brush_Pack Folder on the C: Drive.

Figure 4.37

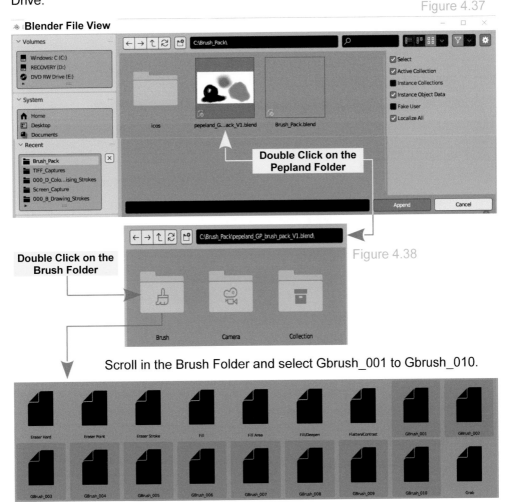

Double Click on the Pepland Folder

Figure 4.38

Double Click on the Brush Folder

Brush   Camera   Collection

Scroll in the Brush Folder and select Gbrush_001 to Gbrush_010.

With the GBrush Files selected (highlighted blue) click Append at the bottom of the Screen.

Figure 4.39   Append   Cancel

With the **GBrush Files** Appended they are added to the Brush selection menu in the Draw Mode 3D Viewport Header in the Brush_Pack.blend file you are working.

Remember: To use the Appended files in the future, you first open the default Blender 2D Animation (Grease Pencil) Application then open Brush_Pack.blend.

Brush Selection menu in the 3D Viewport, draw Mode, Header.

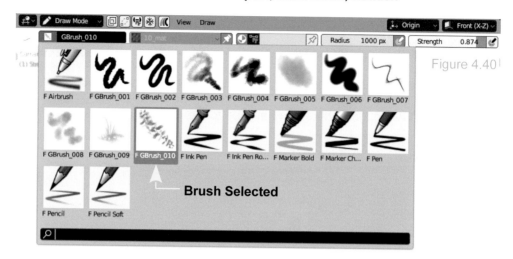

Figure 4.40

Brush Selected

Stroke drawn in the 3D Viewport with Brush **F GBrush_010** selected. (Radius: 1000 px, Strength: 0.874)

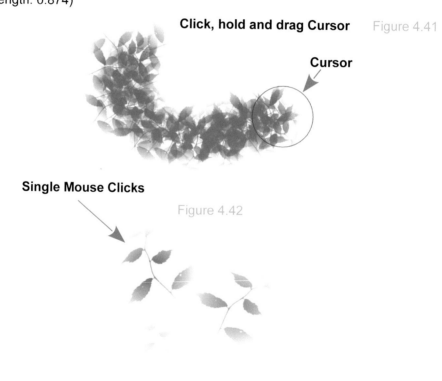

Click, hold and drag Cursor   Figure 4.41

Cursor

Single Mouse Clicks

Figure 4.42

5

The Canvas Explained

5.1 The Canvas

The **Canvas** may be viewed as the Drawing Area in the 3D Viewport Editor which is captured by the Camera.

Figure 5.1

Canvas

Scroll MMB out in the 3D Viewport to see the Canvas.

Press **Num Pad 0** to display the **Camera** (Figure 5.2 L). Click MMB, hold and drag the Mouse and scroll out again to show the Camera pointing towards an imaginary Canvas. In Figure 5.2 R the Canvas has been sketched in the view to show the Camera orientation.

Figure 5.2

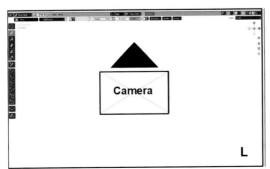

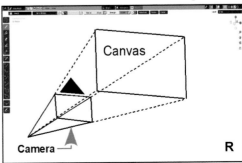

L

R

57

Drawing Strokes in the previous chapters will no doubt give the impression that you are Drawing on a flat white Canvas. It has been explained that this Canvas has Layers and that Strokes (Lines) are Drawn on the separate Layers.

To utilize the full potential of the Grease Pencil you should be aware that this initial perception is misleading.

When you scroll out in the 3D Viewport Editor, the white rectangular area you see is not a drawing area but only that portion of a 3D Environment as seen in the Camera **Camera View.**

Figure 5.3

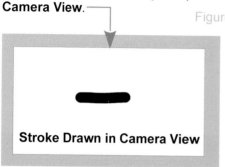

Stroke Drawn in Camera View

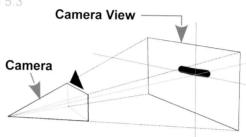

Camera View

Camera

Zoom out in the 3D Viewport. Click MMB, hold and rotate the Viewport to see the Camera pointing toward the Stroke.

Camera View captures a portion of the 3D Environment which will constitute a still image of a Scene or a Frame in an Animation when parts of a Scene are Animated.

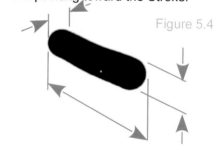

Figure 5.4

Even a **Stroke** (Line) is not what it appears.

By zooming in on the View when it is Rotated you see that the simple Stroke has three dimensions (Figure 5.4).

The default 3D Environment comprises a Three-Dimensional Canvas in which reside two Three-Dimensional Layers. Strokes are Drawn in either of the two Layers.

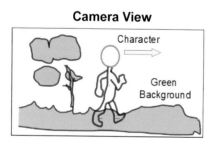

Camera View

Character

Green Background

Figure 5.5

Canvas

Layer 1 **Layer 2**

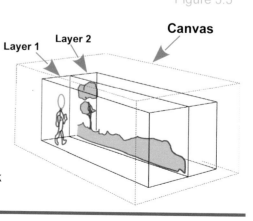

A Character Drawn in one Layer with the Green Background in the second Layer.

The Character would be Animated to walk in the Scene relative to the Background.

In Figure 5.5 the Layers are depicted as cubic volumes inside a Canvas, also a cubic volume. This depiction is purely conceptual to allow you to visualize **Layers in a Canvas** and the Canvas and Layers being three-dimensional.

Note: The Canvas and Layers are NOT cubic volumes but rather infinite space.

The Canvas and Layers are listed in the **Outliner Editor** at the upper RH of the Screen (Figure 5.6).

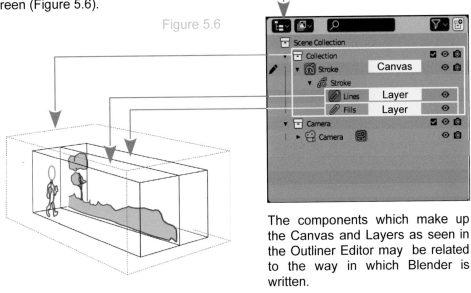

Figure 5.6

The components which make up the Canvas and Layers as seen in the Outliner Editor may be related to the way in which Blender is written.

Blender is written in the **Python** programming language which simplistically is made up from blocks of code (Data or Datablocks) assembled to carry out functions. Functions produce what you see on the computer Screen.

In the **Outliner Editor** each entry (line) represents a **Datablock**. There are Datablocks within Datablocks (Sub-Datablocks).

For example, in the default Grease Pencil, **Outliner Editor,** the entry named **Stroke** is the Datablock for the **Canvas**. The entries named **Lines and Fills** are Datablocks within the Canvas Datablock (Sub-Datablocks). The **Layers are** named **Lines and Fills**.

Note: The Layers reside within a Sub-Datablock named **Stroke**.

Camera is another Datablock which contains data for producing the Camera View.

5.2 Strokes in Layers

When Drawing Strokes as described in Chapter 2, Layers were disregarded. The Drawing procedure is the same for all Layers. When constructing a Scene, you will have to decide which Layer to choose.

Be aware that a Scene can have more than two Layers and more than one Canvas. In fact, in a complex Scene, there can be multiple Canvases with multiple Layers.

5.3 Selecting Layers

To select a **Layer** you click on one of the Datablocks in the **Outliner Editor** or in the **Layer Menu** in the **3D Viewport Editor in Draw Mode**.

Figure 5.7

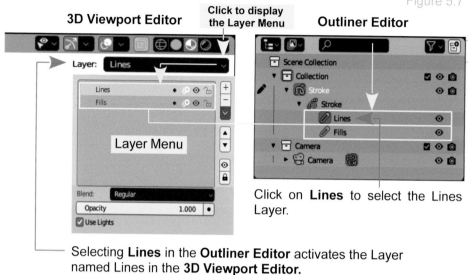

Selecting **Lines** in the **Outliner Editor** activates the Layer named Lines in the **3D Viewport Editor.**

Click on **Lines** to select the Lines Layer.

You may also select the **Layer** in the **3D Viewport Layer Menu**

5.4 Renaming Layers, Lines and Fills

Figure 5.8

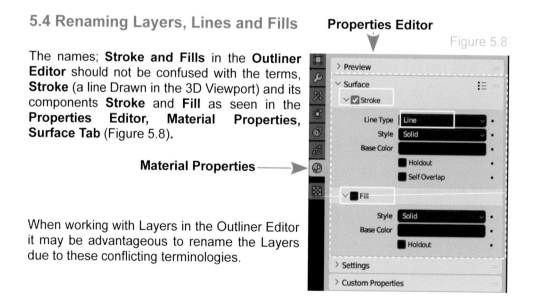

The names; **Stroke and Fills** in the **Outliner Editor** should not be confused with the terms, **Stroke** (a line Drawn in the 3D Viewport) and its components **Stroke** and **Fill** as seen in the **Properties Editor, Material Properties, Surface Tab** (Figure 5.8).

Material Properties

When working with Layers in the Outliner Editor it may be advantageous to rename the Layers due to these conflicting terminologies.

When drawing **Strokes** they are said to have components **Lines and Fills**. In the **Outliner Editor**, Lines and Fills refer to the Layers in a Canvas and the Canvas itself is named **Stroke.** Examine Figure 5.9 following.

Note: You may rename components in Blender making them relevant to the project.

To rename an entry in the **Outliner Editor** double click on the entry to highlight and display the Typing Cursor (Blue Line). Backspace or Delete, type a new name and press Enter on the Keyboard.

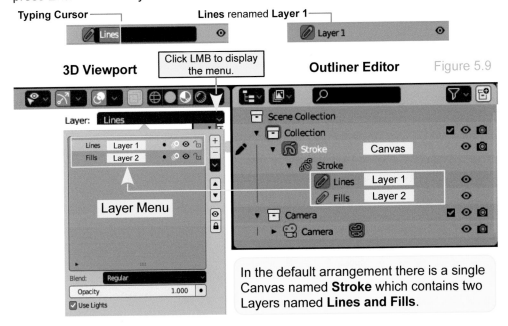

Typing Cursor

Lines renamed **Layer 1**

3D Viewport

Click LMB to display the menu.

Outliner Editor

Figure 5.9

Layer Menu

In the default arrangement there is a single Canvas named **Stroke** which contains two Layers named **Lines and Fills**.

Note: You **can not** rename **Layers** in the **Layer Menu** but you can rename Layers in the **Properties Editor, Object Data Properties, Layers Panel**. You may also rename the Canvas.

5.5 Drawing Strokes in Layers

To **Draw a Stroke** in the 3D Viewport you select one of the Layers. The Layers may be selected in the Outliner Editor or from the Layer menu in the upper RH corner of the 3D Viewport (Figure 5.9).

Note: In the **Outliner Editor** you can rename items to something meaningful to your project. In Figure 5.10 the **Layers** in the Canvas named Stroke have been renamed **Lines_Red_Circle** and **Fills_Green_Circle**. Circle Strokes have been drawn in the 3D Viewport using the Circle Tool after selecting each Layer in turn.

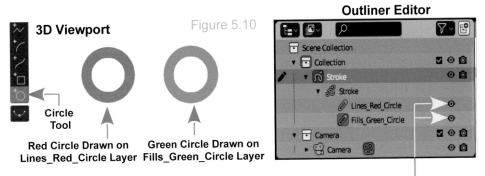

3D Viewport

Figure 5.10

Outliner Editor

Circle Tool

Red Circle Drawn on Lines_Red_Circle Layer   **Green Circle Drawn on Fills_Green_Circle Layer**

To verify and check which Circle Stroke is on which Layer, click the **Eye Icon** in the **Outliner Editor** to Hide / Show the Stroke in the 3D Viewport.

Rotate and Zoom the 3D Viewport to show the Strokes relative to the Camera.

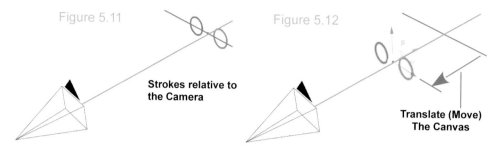

Figure 5.11   Figure 5.12

Strokes relative to the Camera

Translate (Move) The Canvas

Change the 3D Viewport to **Object Mode, click on a Stroke** and using the **Move Tool**, Translate the Strokes towards the Camera. This operation is Translating (Moving) the **Stroke_Canvas** towards the Camera (Figure 5.12).

In **Object Mode**, clicking on one Stroke selects all Strokes since you are selecting the Canvas.

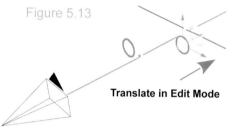

Figure 5.13

With the Canvas and its Strokes repositioned (Figure 5.12) change the 3D Viewport to **Edit Mode**.

Translate in Edit Mode

Click LMB on the Green Circle Stroke to select it and using the Move Tool, Translate the Green Circle away from the Camera. This moves the Green Circle in the **Green_Circle_Layer** (Figure 5.13).

Summary: Object Mode - Select and Move the Canvas. Edit Mode - Select and Move individual Strokes in a Layer. Selecting individual Strokes and Translating does not move a Layer.

Change the 3D Viewport to **Object Mode**. Click LMB on either Circle Stroke (selects all Strokes since you are selecting the Canvas). Moving the **Canvas** moves all Strokes / Layers (Figure 5.14).

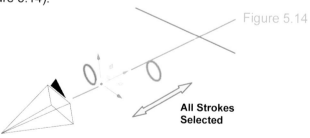

Figure 5.14

All Strokes Selected

Think of the Canvas as an infinite entity not a fixed flat surface or cubic volume but rather an infinite volume of space. In Figure 5.5 the Canvas is depicted as a cubic volume but in fact it is an infinite volume of space. Similarly, Layers are also infinite volumes of space. When a Stroke is Drawn it is created in an infinite Layer which is in an infinite Canvas. In the default 3D Workspace, what you see in the 3D Viewport Editor, is only what the Camera sees (Camera View). The Canvas and Layers extend infinitely.

Figure 5.15 depicts Layers as flat Planes inside a Canvas Volume since this is easier to envisage. Bear in mind that both are infinite. In Figure 5.15 the intention is to show that, when one Layer is placed further away from the Camera, **Camera View** will see more of the Layer which is furthest away. It also shows that a Layer may be Rotated and that Camera View will capture a wider part of the Layer which is furthest away.

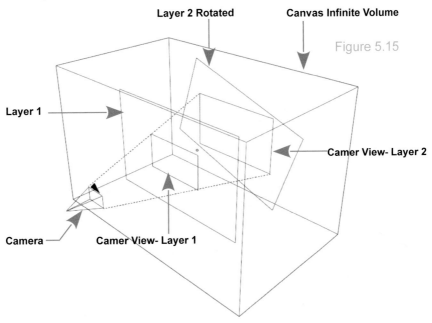

How to position and orientate Layers in a Canvas is described in Chapter 6 in terms of **Placing Strokes** since constructing a Character, Model or Scene Background is the primary objective.

When a Stroke is Drawn it is Drawn in a Layer. **In Object Mode** the Layer may be moved and rotated in 3D Space relative to the Camera. The Stroke itself may be moved and rotated, in **Edit Mode**, relative to the Layer

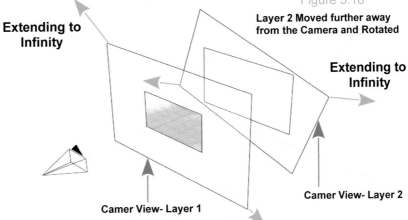

To dispel the concept that a Canvas is a flat plane, think of Layers existing in a Canvas that is infinite. Remember that Layers are also infinite in three dimensions and not flat plan areas.

Strokes in Layers

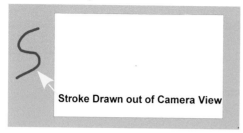

Stroke Drawn out of Camera View

Strokes are Drawn **in a Layer** rather than **on a Layer** and you only see them in the default 3D Viewport when they are in Camera View.

Figure 5.17

Rendering a View with the Stroke drawn outside of Camera View sees only a blank image.

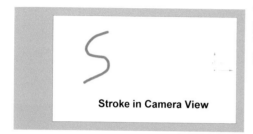

Stroke in Camera View

When the Canvas is moved in Object Mode bringing the Stroke into Camera View the Stroke will display in the Render.

Figure 5.18

When the Layer is moved in the Canvas further away from the Camera it displays smaller in Camera View since the Camera View is a Perspective View.

Figure 5.19

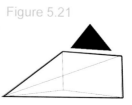

How Do You Move a Canvas?

As previously explained the Canvas is Moved (Translated) with the 3D Viewport in **Object Mode** by selecting Strokes in the 3D Viewport. Clicking a single Stroke selects all Strokes since you are, in fact, selecting the Canvas.

Figure 5.20

◀ **Camera View**.

Remember, what you see is only that part of the Infinite Canvas captured by the Camera (Figure 5.21).

Camera View

Figure 5.21

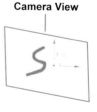

The default Grease Pencil Workspace has one Canvas which has Two Layers.

You may add Layers to the Canvas and you may add Canvases to the Scene.

5.6 Adding Layers

Click LMB to display the **Layers Menu** (Draw Mode).

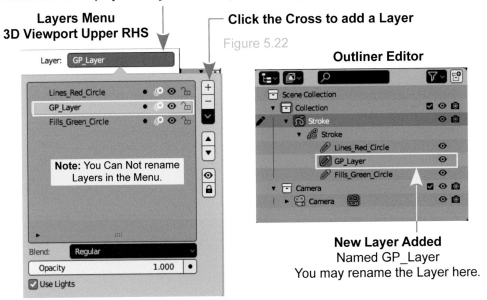

Layers Menu
3D Viewport Upper RHS

Click the Cross to add a Layer

Figure 5.22

Outliner Editor

New Layer Added
Named GP_Layer
You may rename the Layer here.

Clicking the Cross at the RHS of the **Layers Menu** adds a Layer. By default it is named **GP_Layer**. In the **Outliner Editor** rename the Layer to suit your project.

5.7 Layers in the Properties Editor

Figure 5.23

Layers are also listed and may be added and deleted in the **Properties Editor, Object Data Properties.**

As you see, in Figure 5.23, the display in the **Properties Editor** replicated the display in the **Layers Menu**.

Layers may be added, deleted and renamed in the **Object Data Properties**. Do not be confused with the **Object Properties**

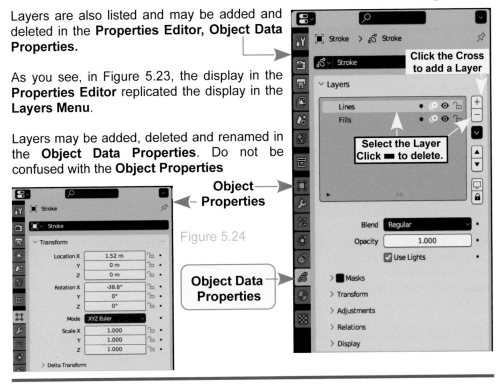

Click the Cross to add a Layer

Select the Layer Click ▬ to delete.

Object — Properties

Figure 5.24

Object Data Properties

5.8 Adding a Canvas

As you have seen in Section 5.3, you may select Layers which reside in the 3D Viewport in the Outliner Editor by clicking on the Datablock in the Outliner Editor. Similarly you may select a Canvas in the **Outliner Editor.**

Adding a Canvas provides another dimension in which to organize work in a Scene.

Figure 5.25

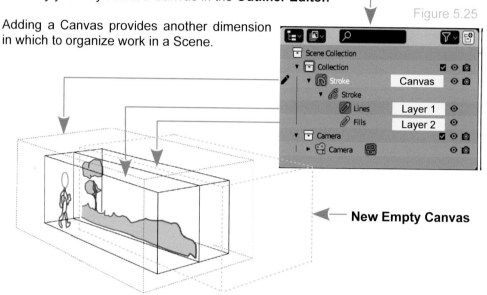

New Empty Canvas

Remember: A Canvas is an infinite volume of 3D Space, not a fixed volume as depicted in the diagram.

If you anticipate that a Scene will become complicated and require this additional dimension of organization, leave the original Canvas with its Layers in situ and create a New Canvas to begin working in. You will then have a Master Canvas (the original) from which to generate further 3D Space if required.

At this point, be aware that additional **Collections** may be created which adds further dimensions.

Figure 5.26

How To Add a Canvas?   **Outliner Editor**

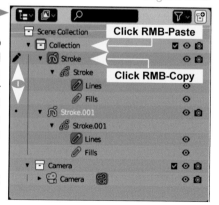

The default Canvas named **Stroke** with its two Layers resides within the Datablocks named Collection. To add a New Canvas, click on **Stroke** (the original Canvas) in the Outliner Editor to select it. RMB click - copy. Click RMB on **Collection** (to select the Collection) then RMB click - paste. A new canvas is added in Collection and named **Stroke.001**.

Note: The **Pencil Icon** adjacent to Stroke and the **Dot** adjacent to Stroke.001.

The **Pencil icon** indicates that Canvas-Stroke is active. To work in the New Canvas (Stroke.001) click on the Dot. The Pencil Icon relocates.

5.9 Adding a Collection

As previously mentioned you may add **Collections** to the Scene providing additional dimensions (3D Spaces) for organizing work.

In the Outliner Editor click on the New Collection button (upper RH corner) to add Collections to the Scene Collection Datablock.

To add Layers to a New Collection, RMB click on Stroke (the Canvas) - select Copy. Click on one of the New Collections - RMB click and paste.

Important: If you have drawn Strokes on Layers in the original Canvas, copying and pasting will duplicate everything to the New Collection.

5.10 Quick Scene Example

Outliner Editor   Figure 5.28

The example shows a simple Scene comprising a Fence, Pathway and Grass.

The three components are Drawn in Draw Mode in different Canvases on the Fills Layer in each Canvas.

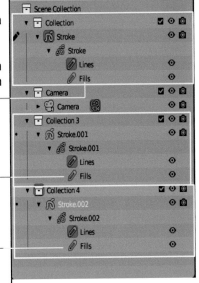

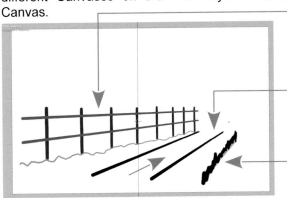

The components have then been Translated and Rotated in Object Mode and Edit Mode selecting the appropriate Stroke Entry in a Collection.

The Camera has been repositioned and orientated to capture the Camera View of the Scene.

By employing this procedure, what would be a complicated exercise, is made relatively simple.

 ◄── **Camera**

3D Viewport Top Orthographic View

5.11 Adding Pre-Constructed Strokes

Blender has a pre-constructed 3D model of a **Monkey** affectionately named **Suzanne** which is used for demonstration purposes. Suzanne is also incorporated in the Grease Pencil in 2D. To find **Suzanne,** open a new **2D Animation Workspace**, change the 3D Viewport Editor to **Object Mode**, click **Add - Grease Pencil** in the **Header** and select **Monkey**.

Note: Make sure you select **Add - Grease Pencil then Monkey**, **NOT** Add - Mesh - Monkey. Adding **Mesh Monkey** introduces a 3D Model which is a different kettle of fish.

2D Animation Workspace - 3D Viewport - Object Mode

Figure 5.29

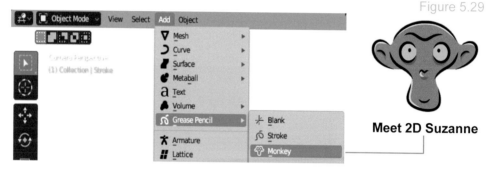

Meet 2D Suzanne

Figure 5.30

When **Suzanne** is entered she is placed in the 3D Viewport as a **New Stroke** and entered in the **Outliner Editor** appropriately named <u>Suzanne</u> (Figure 5.30).

Clicking the **Eye Icons** for the Layers in the **Properties Editor**, **Object Data Properties Tab**, shows that the Stroke, Fills and Lines are on different Layers (Figure 5.31).

Outliner Editor

Figure 5.31

Properties Editor→

Lines Hidden

Fills Hidden

Object Data Properties →

Click the Eye Icons
To Hide Show
Strokes in Layers

By selecting each Layer in turn and investigating the **Materials Properties** in the Properties Editor, it shows Suzanne has been constructed using different **Stroke Types.**

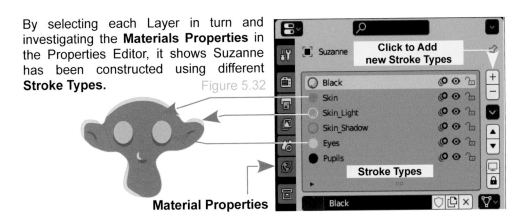

Figure 5.32

Material Properties

5.12 Appending Stroke Properties

Section 5.11 has demonstrated how to add pre-constructed Strokes for use in a Scene. You may also **Append Stroke Properties** which you have created and saved in other Blender Grease Pencil Files. The following exercise shows how to Append from a file and how to use the **Appended Stroke Properties**.

Note: Appending Stroke Properties does NOT mean you append a Stroke that has been previously drawn, rather, you are Appending the **Properties of that Stroke** (i.e. the colors of Line and Fill).

Create a New Blender File. In a new 2D Animation Workspace with the 2D Viewport Editor in Object Mode, add a Monkey (Figure 5.29) and create two new **Stroke Types** (Materials and Material.001) in the **Material Properties** (Figures 5.32, 5.33).

Using the new Stroke Types, Draw Strokes in the 3D Viewport (Figure 5.33).

Figure 5.33

Material - Stroke   **Material Properties**

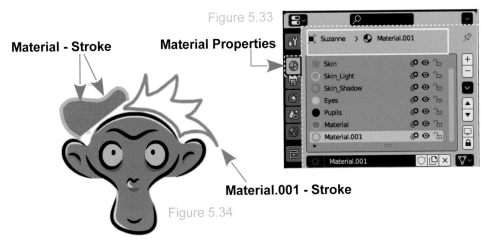

Material.001 - Stroke

Figure 5.34

Save the Blender File. Make a note of where the file is saved and what you named the file. On my PC the Blender file is named **Appended_Strokes.blend** which is saved on the C: Drive in a **Folder** named **Construction_Stuff.**

Figure 5.35

C:\$_A_Blender_GP_2nd_Edition\005_E_The_Canvas_Explained\Construction_Stuff\

Creating the Blender File simply provides a known source to Append into a Scene.

Go ahead and open a new 2D Animation Workspace and create a simple Scene. The Scene can be anything you want. Figure 5.36 represents a Scene with three Strokes drawn using the **Color Attribute** color scheme, the Stroke Type being Solid Stroke with the F Pencil Brush.

Figure 5.36   **Scene Containing Three Strokes**

To Append the Stroke Type Properties you have saved and use them to draw new Strokes in the Scene, click **File** in the **Screen Header** then click **Append** in the menu to open **Blender File View** (Blender's inbuilt File Browser).

In the File Browser you navigate through your file system and find the Blender File containing the Stroke Types you wish to Append (see Chapter 19 titled **Navigate and Save**).

File Path to the Blender File ⎯   Figure 5.37

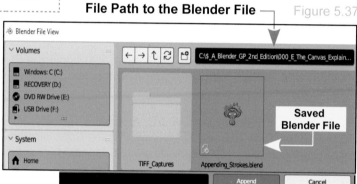

Double click on the file or <u>click on **Append**</u> at the bottom of the panel.

Figure 5.38

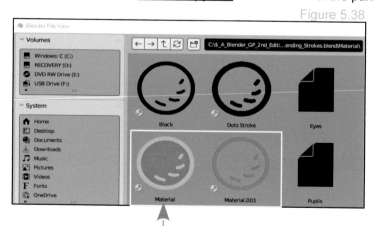

Double Click on Material to display the contents of the Material Folder which contains your Stroke Properties named **Material** and **Material.001**

Go to the **Properties Editor, Material Properties** and add a new **Stroke Channel** (click the Cross in Figure 5.39).

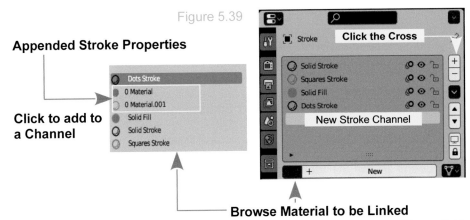

Appended Stroke Properties

Click to add to a Channel

Figure 5.39

Click the Cross

New Stroke Channel

Browse Material to be Linked

Figure 5.40

Click the **Browse Material to be Linked button** and select one of your Appended Stroke Properties to insert it in the New Stroke Channel. Repeat the procedure for the second Stroke Property.

With the new Stroke Properties added to the **Properties Editor, Material Properties** you may select a Property to Draw Strokes in the 3D Viewport.

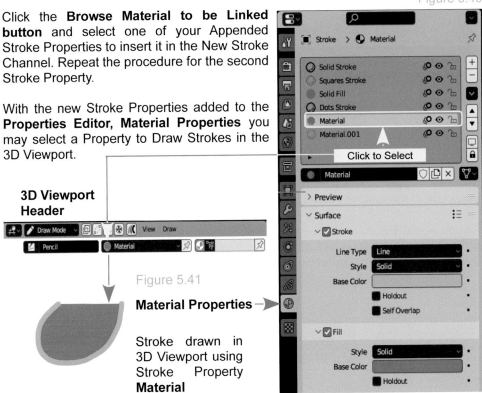

3D Viewport Header

Figure 5.41

Material Properties →

Stroke drawn in 3D Viewport using Stroke Property **Material**

Click to Select

Providing you have a Blender File saved in which you have added the Monkey Suzanne you will be able to Append the Stroke Properties used to draw Suzanne.

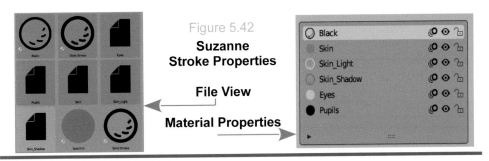

Figure 5.42

Suzanne Stroke Properties

File View

Material Properties

5.13 Appending Scene Content

Appending Properties is not limited to Appending Material Stroke Properties. You may Append anything from a Saved Blender File. For example, if Suzanne has been added to a Scene and new Strokes have been drawn and the Blender File saved (Appending_Strokes_01.blend) the saved file will contain a new Datablock named **Collection.001** as seen in the **Outliner Editor** (Figure 5.43).

Appending Content

New Datablock ——————— Figure 5.43

Scene in the 3D Viewport with Suzanne added and new Strokes Drawn.

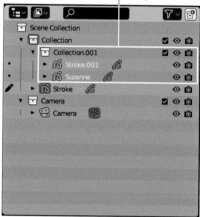

With the Blender File saved and a new 2D Animation Workspace opened (3D Viewport empty) go to the **Screen Header** and click on **File - Append** to open **Blender File View**. Navigate to the saved Blender File (Appending_Strokes_01.blend).

As you see in Figure 5.44, Suzanne and the new Strokes are listed in the **Outliner Editor** under **Collection.001** (Stroke.001 and Suzanne). In **Blender File View**, shift select **Collection and Collection.001** and click **Append**.

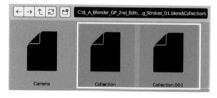

Figure 5.44

The Datablocks are Appended to the current Blender File (the new 2D Workspace) and entered in the **Outliner Editor** as **Collection.002**.

Figure 5.45

Suzanne complete with modifications displays in the 3D Viewport.

Placing Strokes

The spacial arrangement of the 3D Viewport with its Collections, Canvases and Layers simplifies the creation of complex Scenes. To assist when placing Strokes relative to other Strokes in the Scene visual references are provided.

By rotating the default 3D Viewport and zooming out you see the Camera pointing into 3D Space. There is no reference point, other than the Camera, which allows you to position a Stroke in the Scene.

6.1 Scene Axis

The **X, Y and Z Axes** of the Scene may be displayed by activating controls in the **Viewport Overlays**.

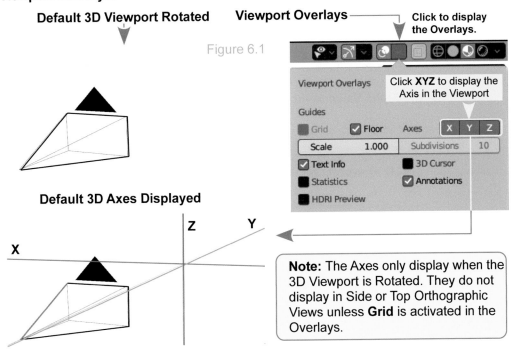

Default 3D Viewport Rotated

Viewport Overlays — Click to display the Overlays.

Figure 6.1

Viewport Overlays — Click **XYZ** to display the Axis in the Viewport

Guides

Grid ☑ Floor Axes X Y Z

Scale 1.000 Subdivisions 10

☑ Text Info ■ 3D Cursor

■ Statistics ☑ Annotations

■ HDRI Preview

Default 3D Axes Displayed

Z Y

X

Note: The Axes only display when the 3D Viewport is Rotated. They do not display in Side or Top Orthographic Views unless **Grid** is activated in the Overlays.

With **Grid** activated in the Overlays the XYZ Axes display in the Top, Side and Front Orthographic Views with a Grid displayed in the Viewport. When the Viewport is Rotated the Axes remain displayed but the Grid disappears.

6.2 Viewport Grid Floor

To display a **Grid Floor** when the **Viewport** is Rotated you activate **Floor** in the **Overlays**.

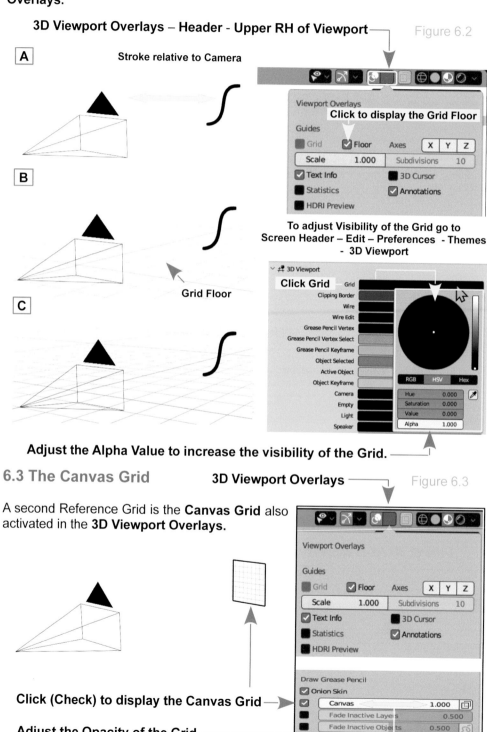

3D Viewport Overlays – Header - Upper RH of Viewport

Figure 6.2

A

Stroke relative to Camera

Viewport Overlays

Click to display the Grid Floor

Guides

☐ Grid   ☑ Floor   Axes   X   Y   Z

Scale   1.000   Subdivisions   10

☑ Text Info   ☐ 3D Cursor

☐ Statistics   ☑ Annotations

☐ HDRI Preview

B

To adjust Visibility of the Grid go to Screen Header – Edit – Preferences - Themes - 3D Viewport

Grid Floor

∨ ⚓ 3D Viewport

Click Grid   Grid

Clipping Border

Wire

Wire Edit

Grease Pencil Vertex

Grease Pencil Vertex Select

Grease Pencil Keyframe

Object Selected

Active Object

Object Keyframe

Camera

Empty

Light

Speaker

C

RGB   HSV   Hex

Hue   0.000

Saturation   0.000

Value   0.000

Alpha   1.000

Adjust the Alpha Value to increase the visibility of the Grid.

6.3 The Canvas Grid

3D Viewport Overlays

Figure 6.3

A second Reference Grid is the **Canvas Grid** also activated in the **3D Viewport Overlays.**

Viewport Overlays

Guides

☐ Grid   ☑ Floor   Axes   X   Y   Z

Scale   1.000   Subdivisions   10

☑ Text Info   ☐ 3D Cursor

☐ Statistics   ☑ Annotations

☐ HDRI Preview

Draw Grease Pencil

☑ Onion Skin

☑   Canvas   1.000

☐   Fade Inactive Layers   0.500

☐   Fade Inactive Objects   0.500

Vertex Paint

Opacity   1.000

Click (Check) to display the Canvas Grid →

Adjust the Opacity of the Grid

When activated the **Canvas Grid** displays as a rather insignificant little square in the Viewport.

Figure 6.4

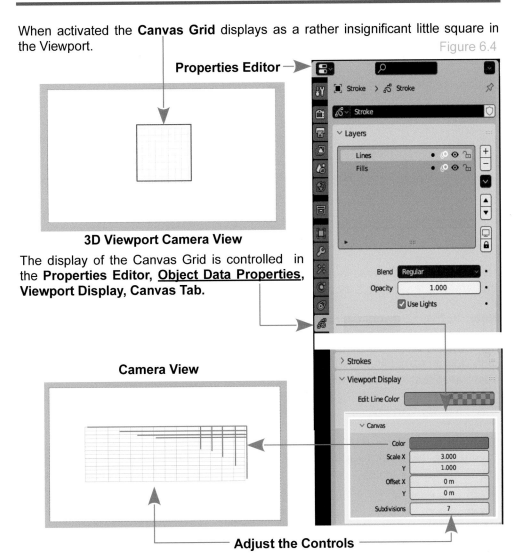

Properties Editor

3D Viewport Camera View

The display of the Canvas Grid is controlled in the **Properties Editor, <u>Object Data Properties</u>, Viewport Display, Canvas Tab.**

Camera View

Adjust the Controls

6.4 Header Placement Controls

Figure 6.5

Controls are located in the **3D Viewport Header** with the <u>**default settings**</u> being **Origin, Front (X-Y) and Guides** (Guides inactive).

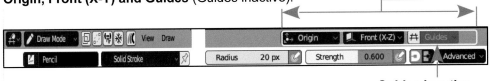

Guides Inactive

With a Stroke drawn in the 3D Viewport using the default **Stroke Placement** settings in **Draw Mode**, the Stroke is drawn on the **X- Z Plane** relative to the **Origin**.

The **Origin** is an arbitrary point coinciding with the center of the **Canvas** (Figure 6.6).

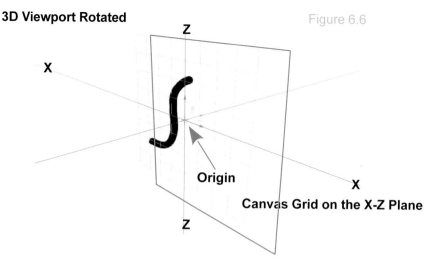

3D Viewport Rotated

Figure 6.6

Z

X

Origin

X

Canvas Grid on the X-Z Plane

Z

Remember: The **Canvas** is the 3D Space containing Layers not the white rectangle that you see in Camera View.

Note: In Blender every Object has an **Origin** (Center of Geometry). In the Grease Pencil the Origin is the Center of Geometry of the **Canvas** and only displays in the 3D Viewport in Object Mode and Edit Mode. Origins do not display for Layers or individual Strokes although, in Edit Mode, selecting one of the transform Tools in the Tool Panel sees a Manipulation Widget locate at the Origin of a Stroke.

6.5 The 3D Cursor

3D Viewport Overlays

Figure 6.7

Although not strictly a Placement Tool the 3D Cursor may be positioned in the 3D Viewport to act as a reference point.

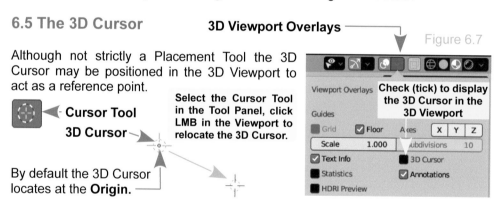

Cursor Tool

Select the Cursor Tool in the Tool Panel, click LMB in the Viewport to relocate the 3D Cursor.

3D Cursor

By default the 3D Cursor locates at the **Origin.**

6.6 The Origin

As stated above, every Object has an **Origin**. Selecting one of the transform Tools in the Tool Panel (in Edit Mode) sees a **Manipulation Widget** locate at the **Origin of a Stroke.**

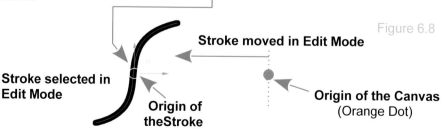

Figure 6.8

Stroke moved in Edit Mode

Stroke selected in Edit Mode

Origin of theStroke

Origin of the Canvas (Orange Dot)

When **Drawing a Stroke in Draw Mode** after repositioning the 3D Cursor the Origin of the Stroke does not locate at the position of the 3D Cursor.

Conversely, adding a **Grease Pencil Stroke** (Pre-prepared Stroke) in **Object Mode** (Select Add in the Viewport Header - Grease Pencil - Stroke) the Stroke does locate at the position of the 3D Cursor.

Figure 6.9

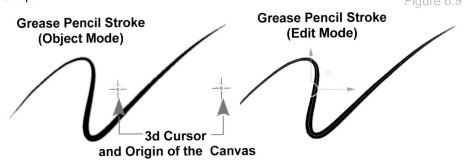

Grease Pencil Stroke (Object Mode)

Grease Pencil Stroke (Edit Mode)

3d Cursor and Origin of the Canvas

In **Edit Mode** you can **Translate the Stroke** relative to its Origin.

Figure 6.10

6.7 Changing the Placement Controls

When changing the Settings from Front (X -Z) to Side (Y - Z) Strokes are Drawn on the **Y - Z Plane.**

3D Viewport Rotated

Strokes Drawn with Side (Y-Z) set are Drawn on the Y-Z Plane in the Viewport not the Plane of the View.

X-Y Plane
Plane of the View

Viewport Rotated.

Y-Z Plane

Y Axis and Z Axis Aligned

Strokes on the Y – Z Plane

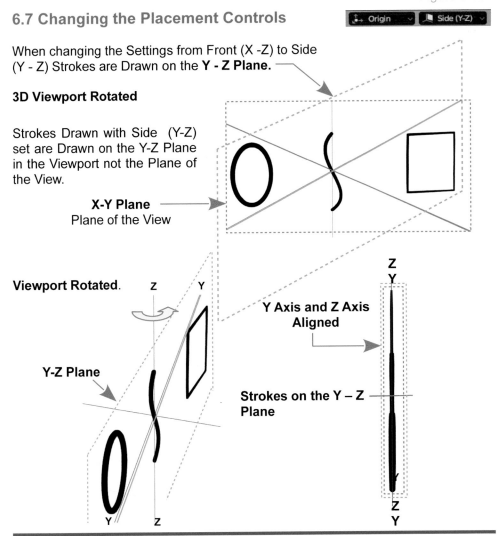

Strokes Drawn with **Top X -Y** selected are Drawn on the X - Y Plane in **Top Orthographic View**.

With **Cursor** selected and the 3D Cursor display activated in the Overlays, Strokes are Drawn on a Plane designated by the location of the Cursor when the 3D View is Rotated.   Figure 6.11

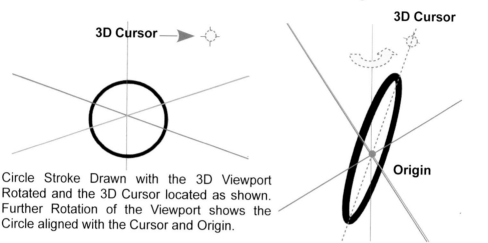

Circle Stroke Drawn with the 3D Viewport Rotated and the 3D Cursor located as shown. Further Rotation of the Viewport shows the Circle aligned with the Cursor and Origin.

6.8 Stroke Placement Options

In demonstrating Stroke Placement to this point the different Drawing Plane options have been employed with the **Stroke Placement** being the **Origin**. The following will show Stroke Placement options.

3D Cursor   Figure 6.12

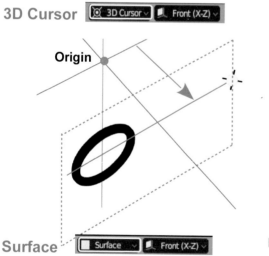

Using **Stroke Placement, 3D Cursor** sees a Stroke Drawn on a Plane which is positioned at the location of the 3D Cursor relative to the Origin.

Note: The Plane is orientated on the **Front X – Y Plane.**

Surface   Figure 6.13

With **Surface Stroke Placement** activated, a Stroke drawn in the 2D Viewport Editor in Draw Mode will attach to the surface of a Mesh Object placed in the Scene.

To demonstrate, add a **Mesh Cube Object** to the default 2D Viewport Editor in **Object Mode**.   Figure 6.14

Cube Object entered in the 3D Viewport which has been Rotated and the Cube Scaled down. With the Cube selected (orange outline), in the **Properties Editor**, Material Properties give the Cube a pale blue color.

Figure 6.15

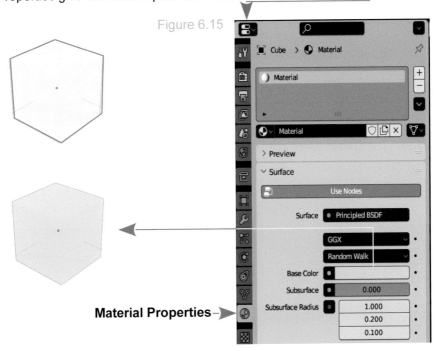

Material Properties→

Change the 3D Viewport from Object Mode to Draw Mode.

Note: With the 3D Viewport in Object Mode after entering the Cube Object, you will find that there is no **Draw Mode** option available when you click on **Object Mode** in the Header. The Viewport has reverted to Blender's **3D Modeling Workspace**.

Figure 6.16

In the Outliner Editor you will see that Cube has been entered as a new Datablock in the Canvas named Collection. The new Datablock contains the information to display the 3D Model of the Cube Object.

To use the Cube Object in the 2D Environment and continue to Draw Strokes you change to the 2D Workspace by selecting the Datablock named **Stroke** in the Outliner Editor. With the Datablock named Stroke selected the Draw Mode option is reinstated in the **3D Viewport Editor Header** display options.

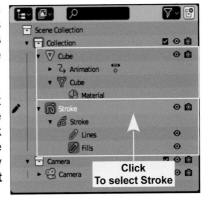

Figure 6.17

79

With the 3D Viewport Rotated draw a horizontal Stroke across the face of the Cube. Rotate the Viewport to see the Stroke conforming to the shape of the Cube Surface.

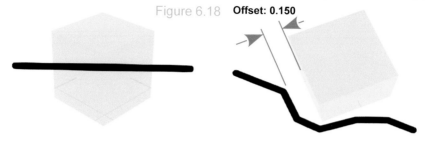

Figure 6.18   Offset: 0.150

Note: The **Offset** value in the Stroke Placement menu.

Offset: 0.000

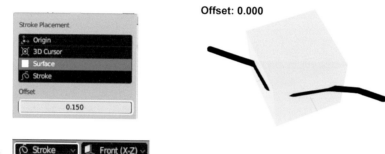

Stroke

Combining the **Stroke Placement** options and **Drawing Plane** options assists when you want a precise Stroke orientation. To understand how this works follow this exercise:

Step 1: In the default 2D Viewport Editor, Camera View, activate the display of the 3D Cursor and the Canvas Grid in the Overlays menu. In draw Mode, draw a Stroke as shown in Figure 6.19.

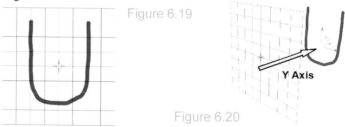

Figure 6.19

Y Axis

Figure 6.20

Step 2: Rotate the Viewport and in **Edit Mode**, select the Stroke. Using the Move Tool, Translate the Stroke along the **Y Axis** (Figure 6.20).

Figure 6.21

Step 3: Change back to **Camera View** (Num Pad 0) in **Draw Mode** and change the Stroke Placement control **Origin** to **Stroke**.

Note: When selecting **Stroke** you have **Target All Point** options.

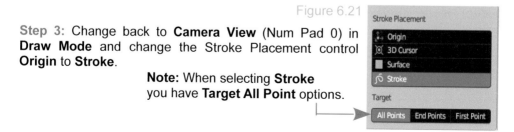

Step 4: Draw a second Stroke.   Figure 6.22

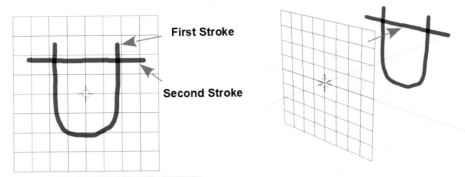

First Stroke

Second Stroke

Caveat: At the time of writing the Placement Option: **Stroke** is described using Blender version 3.5.0.

Rotating the Viewport shows the second Stroke located at the plane of the first Stroke.

Step 5: Change back to Camera View and change Stroke Placement **Stroke** to **Origin**. Draw a third Stroke.

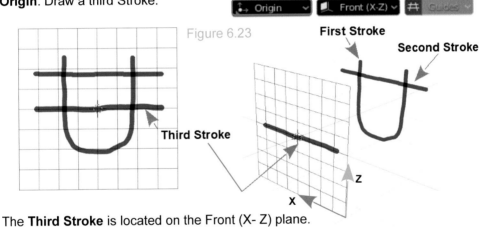

Figure 6.23

First Stroke

Second Stroke

Third Stroke

Z

X

The **Third Stroke** is located on the Front (X- Z) plane.

Step 6: Change to Side View (Num Pad 3) (Figure 6.25), and relocate the 3D Cursor between the Strokes previously Drawn. Change Stroke placement to **3D Cursor**.

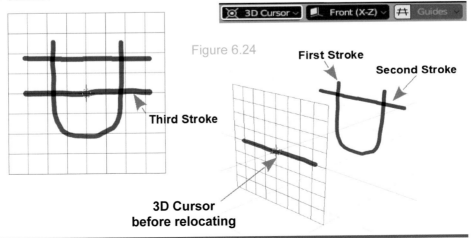

Figure 6.24

First Stroke

Second Stroke

Third Stroke

3D Cursor before relocating

In Camera View draw a Fourth Stroke (Figure 6.26).

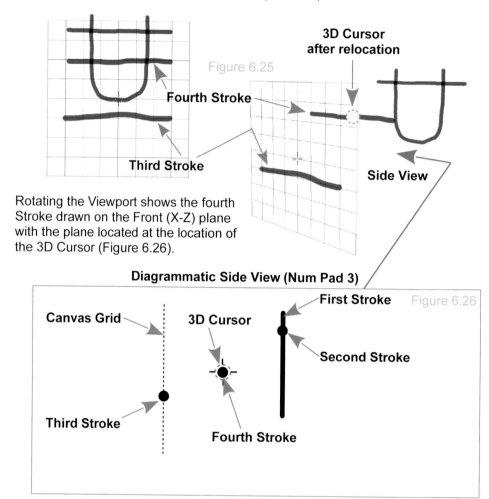

Figure 6.25

3D Cursor
after relocation

Fourth Stroke

Third Stroke

Side View

Rotating the Viewport shows the fourth
Stroke drawn on the Front (X-Z) plane
with the plane located at the location of
the 3D Cursor (Figure 6.26).

Diagrammatic Side View (Num Pad 3)

Figure 6.26

First Stroke

Canvas Grid

3D Cursor

Second Stroke

Third Stroke

Fourth Stroke

6.9 Aligning to a Plane

In the preceding examples the Strokes that have been drawn have been primarily
aligned on the X - Y Plane. Remember the **options.**

To Draw a Stroke aligned to one of the options have the
3D Viewport in the corresponding View. For example,
to Draw a Stroke aligned to the Top (X - Y) Plane, have
the 3D Viewport in Top Orthographic View (Num Pad
7).

Origin   Front (X-Z)   Guide

Drawing Plane

View
Front (X-Z)
Side (Y-Z)
Top (X-Y)
Cursor

Figure 6.27

Top Orthographic View
(Num Pad 7)

Camera View
(Num Pad 0)

User Perspective View
(Rotate Viewport)

6.10 Drawing Guides

To assist when drawing Strokes a selection of **Guide Lines** may be drawn.

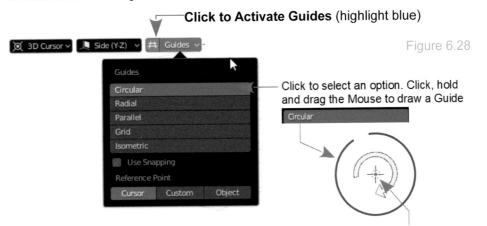

┌───**Click to Activate Guides** (highlight blue)

Figure 6.28

Click to select an option. Click, hold and drag the Mouse to draw a Guide

Circle Guide located at the position of the 3**Origin**

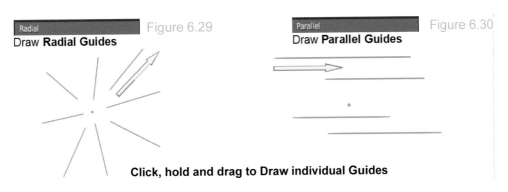

Figure 6.29
Draw **Radial Guides**

Figure 6.30
Draw **Parallel Guides**

Click, hold and drag to Draw individual Guides

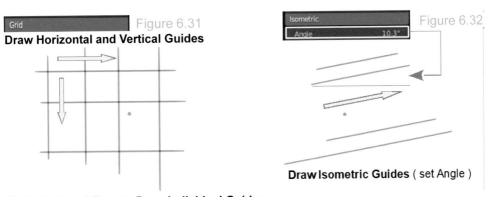

Figure 6.31
Draw Horizontal and Vertical Guides

Figure 6.32
Draw Isometric Guides (set Angle)

Click, Hold and Drag to Draw individual Guides

7

Stroke Effects

Stroke Effects are non-destructive ways of altering the appearance of Strokes which have been drawn in the 3D Viewport Editor. They are said to be a special set of Viewport real-time visual effects that can be apply to the object.

Remember: Strokes are drawn, primarily, to construct a Character or Scenery for an Animation. What is Drawn in the 3D Viewport is a Frame or Frames in the Animation. The View in the 3D Viewport is Rendered to create a Frame or series of Frames.

These effects treat the object as if it was just an image. For that reason, they have effect on the whole object and can not limit their influence on certain parts like layers, materials or vertex groups, as with modifiers. Also unlike modifiers, they can not be applied to the object.

Their main purpose is to have a quick way to apply visual effects on your drawings like blurring, pixelation, wave distortion, among others.

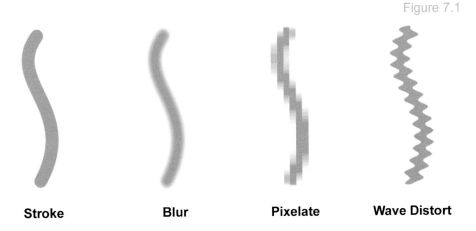

Figure 7.1

| Stroke | Blur | Pixelate | Wave Distort |

Visual Effects are best suited for quick Viewport Visualization.

Important:

Stroke Effects (Figure 7.1) can only be seen with the 3D Viewport in **Rendered Viewport Shading Mode** and when Added they influence all Strokes that are Drawn in a Canvas. They can not be Added to individual Strokes in individual Layers. The Stroke Effect may be Animated to display and change over a series of Frames in an Animation (See Animation Chapter 10).

7.1 Viewport Shading Modes

In the Grease Pencil 2D Workspace there are several Modes for viewing the 3D Viewport (the working space) called **Viewport Shading Modes**. The controls for selecting the Viewing Modes are found in the upper RHS corner of the 3D Viewport in the Header.

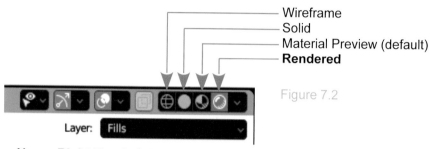

Wireframe
Solid
Material Preview (default)
Rendered

Figure 7.2

Layer: Fills

Upper Right Hand of the 3D Viewport

The default Viewing Mode is Material Preview which has been used when demonstrating Drawing Strokes.

To demonstrate **Stroke Effects** have the **3D Viewport Editor** in **Rendered Viewport Shading Mode** (Figure 7.2).

Figure 7.3

7.2 Adding Stroke Effects   Outliner Editor →

Remember: When a Stroke Effect is Added it affects all Strokes Drawn on all Layers in a Canvas.

> **Pencil Icon** – Indicates that the Canvas named Stroke is active (Strokes may be Drawn in the Layers).

In Figure 7.3 a second Canvas has been added to the Collection (See Chapter 5). Both Canvases have two Layers (Lines and Fills).

Draw a Stroke in the original Canvas named **Stroke** in the **Lines Layer**.

Draw a second Stroke in the **Fills Layer**.

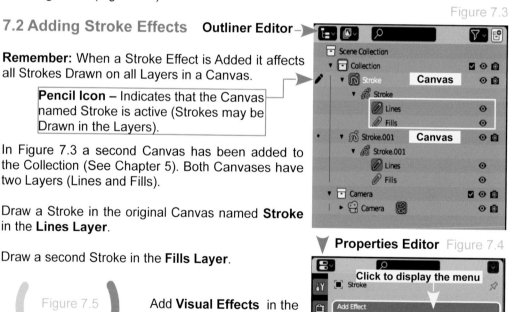

Properties Editor Figure 7.4

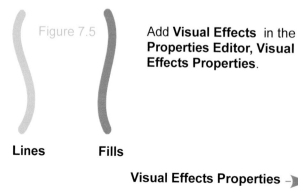

Figure 7.5

Add **Visual Effects** in the **Properties Editor, Visual Effects Properties**.

Lines   **Fills**

Visual Effects Properties →

With Strokes Drawn in the 3D Viewport, in Draw Mode, in the Canvas named Stroke, in Layers, Lines and Fills, click **Add Effect** in the **Visual Effects Properties** and select **Wave Distortion** in the menu.

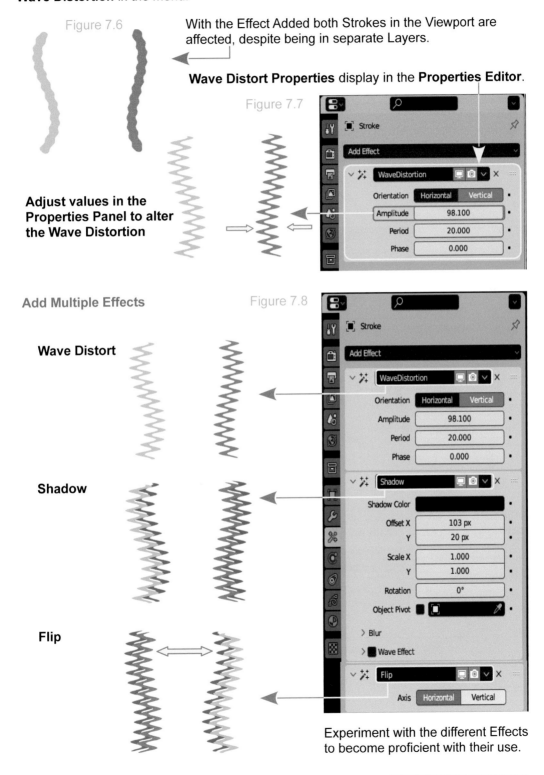

Figure 7.6

With the Effect Added both Strokes in the Viewport are affected, despite being in separate Layers.

Wave Distort Properties display in the **Properties Editor**.

Figure 7.7

Adjust values in the Properties Panel to alter the Wave Distortion

Add Multiple Effects

Figure 7.8

Wave Distort

Shadow

Flip

Experiment with the different Effects to become proficient with their use.

Stroke Effects - Canvas

Outliner Editor ➞

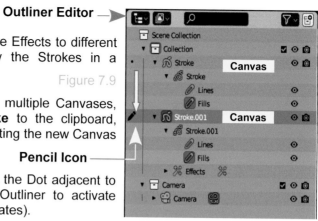

If you wish to Add different Stroke Effects to different Strokes in a Scene you Draw the Strokes in a different Canvas.

Figure 7.9

Remember: If you intend using multiple Canvases, copy the Canvas named **Stroke** to the clipboard, select **Collection** and Paste creating the new Canvas named **Stroke.001**.

Pencil Icon ──────

To draw in the new Canvas click the Dot adjacent to the new Canvas name in the Outliner to activate before Drawing (Pencil Icon relocates).

Figure 7.10

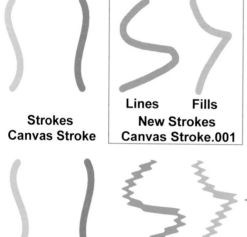

Strokes
Canvas Stroke

Lines **Fills**
New Strokes
Canvas Stroke.001

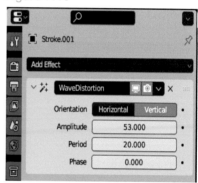

◀──── **Wave Distortion Effect Added**

The Wave Distortion Effect only affects Strokes in Canvas Stroke.001

Figure 7.11

7.3 Adding a Modifier   **Properties Editor** ➞

Although not an Effect as such, a Modifier may be added to a Stroke to create an Effect.

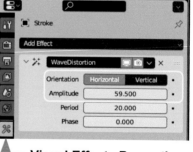

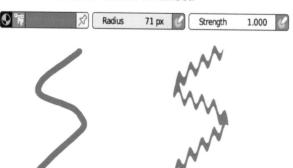

──▲── **Visual Effects Properties**

Note: The Orientation and Amplitude Values

Stroke Drawn in the 3D Viewport with a Wave Distortion Effect Added

To add a Modifier go to the **Properties Editor, Modifier Properties** and click **Add Modifier**.

Select **Multiple Strokes** in the menu.

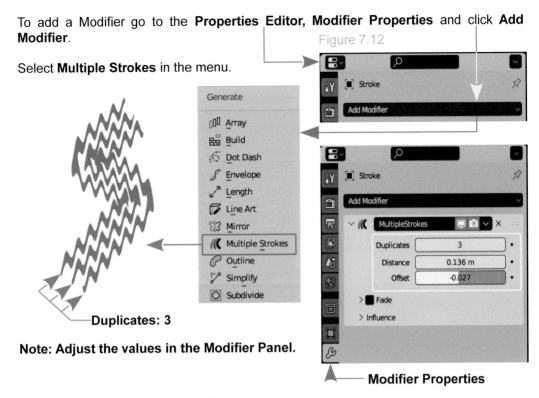

Figure 7.12

Generate
- ▯▯▯ Array
- Build
- Dot Dash
- Envelope
- Length
- Line Art
- Mirror
- Multiple Strokes
- Outline
- Simplify
- Subdivide

Duplicates: 3

Note: Adjust the values in the Modifier Panel.

Modifier Properties

7.4 Stroke Thickness Profile

As with a Modifier the **Thickness Profile Tool** is not strictly a Stroke Effect but it does create an Effect by shaping a Stroke when used in conjunction with one of the Stroke Curve Tools in the Draw Mode Tool Panel.

2D Animation Workspace – Draw Mode

Figure 7.13

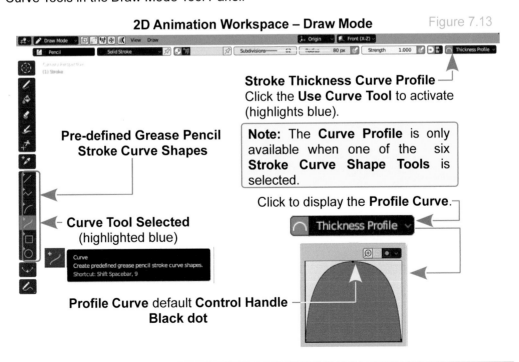

Stroke Thickness Curve Profile
Click the **Use Curve Tool** to activate (highlights blue).

Note: The **Curve Profile** is only available when one of the six **Stroke Curve Shape Tools** is selected.

Pre-defined Grease Pencil Stroke Curve Shapes

Click to display the **Profile Curve.**

Curve Tool Selected
(highlighted blue)

Curve
Create predefined grease pencil stroke curve shapes.
Shortcut: Shift Spacebar, 9

Thickness Profile

Profile Curve default **Control Handle Black dot**

How To use the Profile Curve

Figure 7.14

Control Handles

Control Handles Moved

To Draw the Stroke using the **Curve Tool** - Select the **Curve Tool** in the **Tool Panel,** click, hold and drag the **Mouse in the 3D Viewport,** move Control Handles, press **Enter** to set.

To use the Profile Curve, select the Curve Tool in the Tool Panel. **Before Drawing, activate the Profile Curve** in the 3D Viewport Header. Draw the Stroke.

With the **Profile Curve Active** the profile of the Stroke is determined by the shape of the **Profile Curve**.

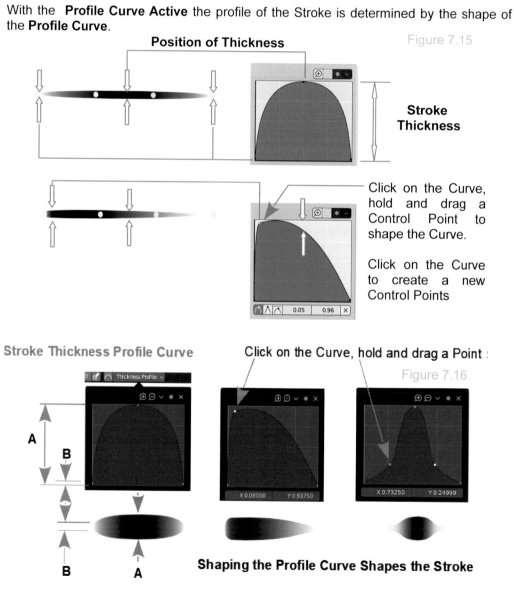

Position of Thickness

Figure 7.15

Stroke Thickness

Click on the Curve, hold and drag a Control Point to shape the Curve.

Click on the Curve to create a new Control Points

Stroke Thickness Profile Curve

Click on the Curve, hold and drag a Point :

Figure 7.16

A

B

X 0.08000   Y 0.93750

X 0.73250   Y 0.24999

B   A

Shaping the Profile Curve Shapes the Stroke

Background Image Tracing

8.1 Tracing

There are no hard and fast rules when it comes to drawing. Whatever suits you and what you are comfortable with is the best way.

One technique, when drawing a character, is to do a rough sketch on one Layer, add a new Layer and draw new Strokes over the original. There are Editing and Smoothing methods which can be applied to produce a professional drawing. Finally delete the first Layer.

For example: Add a new layer in the **Properties Editor, Object Properties, Layers Tab** (GP_Layer Figure 8.1). Click on the Layer to select it.

Draw a sketch on **GP_Layer**.   Figure 8.2

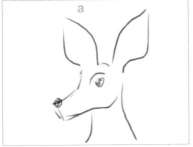

Select the Layer named **Lines** and draw new Strokes tracing over the sketch. Delete the GP_Layer (Figures 8.2 a, b, c).

Properties Editor Figure 8.1

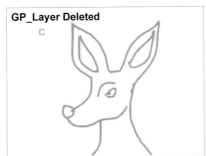

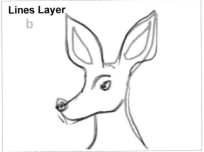

The diagrams in Figure 8.2 leave a lot to be desired in demonstrating a professional drawing but shows the tracing technique. The sketch looks better than the tracing!

Another technique is to draw a sketch on paper, scan the drawing, then enter the scanned image as a template for tracing. This applies to any image saved on the computer. Images entered in Blender may be either a **Background Image** or a **Reference Image**.

Background Images Render as part of the Scene being created. **Reference Images** do not Render and, therefore, are suitable as templates for tracing.

Images can be entered in the Grease Pencil in two ways: **Drag and Drop** or by using the **Add Image Selection Method.**

8.2 Add Image - Selection Method

To Add an Image, change the 3D Viewport from the default Draw Mode to **Object Mode**. In the 3D Viewport Header click **Add**, select **Image**, then select either **Reference** or **Background**. Selecting either opens **Blender File View** where you navigate to the Folder containing your Image (See Chapter 18). Click on the Image to select, then click **Load Reference Image** or **Load Background Image** in the lower RH corner of the Panel.

3D Viewport Header – Upper LHS   Click **Add - Image**   Figure 8.3

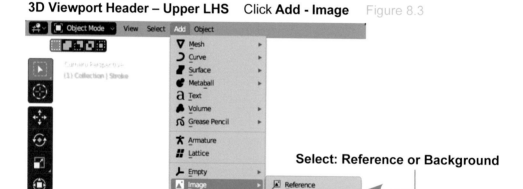

Images Saved on Computer – Blender File View   Figure 8.4

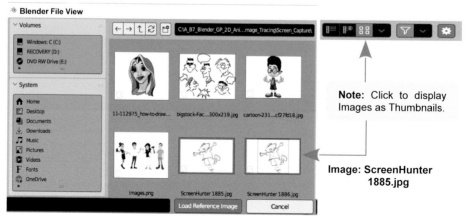

With the Image loaded in the 2D Viewport Editor you will see the file name of the image under **Empty** in the **Outliner Editor**. Figure 8.5

Figure 8.6

Image: ScreenHunter 1885.jpg

Empty is entered as a new **Canvas** in the Scene containing the **Datablock** named ScreenHunter 1885.jpg (See Chapter 5).

Providing you have entered the Image as a **Reference Image**, you select one of the Layers in the Canvas named (Layer: Lines or Layer: Fills), change the 3D Viewport to **Draw Mode** and trace Strokes over the Image.

Note: Draw Mode is not available unless you have selected a Canvas Layer.

When the 3D Viewport is Rendered (Press F12 on the Keyboard) only the Strokes are included in the render.

Before Tracing you can adjust the Image to suit your Strokes. **Select the Image in the Outliner Editor.**

Mouse over on the Image Border, click, hold and drag to scale the image. Figure 8.7

Figure 8.8

Alternatively, click on the Image, S Key drag the Mouse to Scale, R Key Rotate or G Key (Grab) and Translate. Figure 8.9

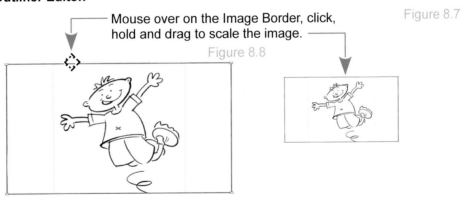

Note: A Reference Image only displays in Camere Perspective View and Front Orthographic View. Tracing the Image may be done in either view but you may find that Strokes Drawn using one of the Pre-defined Stroke Tools from the Tool Panel are hidden behind the Reference Image until Enter is pressed to set the Stroke.

8.3 Drag and Drop Method

The Drag and Drop Method only works with the Viewport in Camera Perspective View and depends on having the Image displayed in an external Image Viewer on a second monitor or by dividing the Screen display. Click on the Image in the external display, hold and drag into the 3D Viewport. **Note:** The image is loaded filling the entire Canvas (Scroll out in Camera Perspective View).

Figure 8.10

When using this method the Image is entered as a **Reference Image** only and you do not have the ability to Scale, Rotate or Translate the image. The Image is not entered in the Outliner Editor.

Change the 3D Viewport to Draw Mode and trace Strokes over the Image. Only the Traced Strokes Render (Figure 8.11).

Figure 8.11

Rendered View

3D Objects

The Grease Pencil, **2D Animation Workspace** operates in Blender's 3D Environment, therefore, 3D Objects may be entered to form part of a Scene or for Stroke construction. In Chapter 6, Figure 6.18 a Cube Object was used to demonstrate **Stroke Placement - Surface.**

Figure 9.1

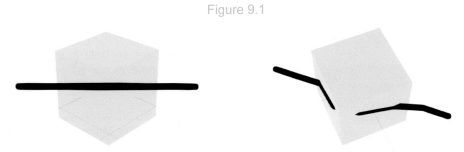

The Cube Object is one of several **Procedural Objects** built into Blender which are accessed in the **3D Viewport Header** with the **Viewport** in **Object Mode**.

Figure 9.2

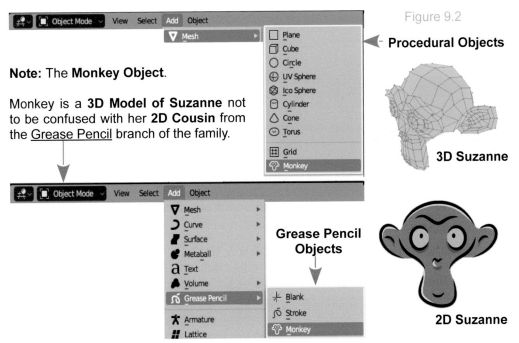

Note: The **Monkey Object**.

Monkey is a **3D Model of Suzanne** not to be confused with her **2D Cousin** from the Grease Pencil branch of the family.

9.1 Adding a 3D Object

When a 3D Object is added to a Scene it is entered as a New **Datablock** in the **Outliner Editor.** The Datablock is not a Canvas and it doesn't have any Layers, therefore, you can not Draw Strokes with the Object selected.

To Draw Strokes you have to be in **Draw Mode** in the **3D Viewport Editor**. After entering Suzanne (or any Procedural Object) the 3D Viewport will be in Object Mode and you will find there is no **Draw Mode** in Mode Selection Menu.

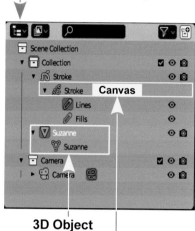

Outliner Editor Figure 9.3

3D Object

Figure 9.4

To Draw Strokes, select the **Stroke Canvas** in the Outliner Editor. The 3D Viewport, Mode selection menu will then display with the **Draw Mode option**.

When 3D Objects are added into the 2D Workspace by default they display as a very pale shade of gray against the white Canvas.

Note: The 3D Viewport is in **Material Preview, Display Mode.**

←—**Draw Mode**

To see Objects with definition, change the Viewport display to **Solid Display.**

Figure 9.5

Material Preview   **Solid**

9.2 Drawing Strokes on Objects

In Chapter 6, Figure 61.8, Surface Placement a 3D Cube Object was added to the Scene and it was demonstrated that a Stroke could be Drawn on the Surface by selecting **Surface Placement** in the 3D Viewport Header.

Figure 9.6

With a Stroke Drawn you see the Stroke conform to the Objects Surface with the **Offset value** set in the Surface Placement menu. By entering Object Mode and deleting the Cube Object you will be left with only the Stroke in the Viewport.

Warning: When changing from Draw Mode to Object Mode, after drawing a Stroke, the **Stroke will be the selected Object**. If you inadvertently delete the **Stroke** from the Viewport at this point you are deleting the **Canvas** from the **Outliner Editor** and will lose the ability to Draw further Strokes.

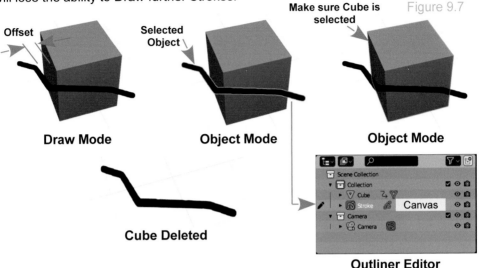

Figure 9.7

Draw Mode

Object Mode

Object Mode

Cube Deleted

Outliner Editor

Another Example

Draw Strokes on the surface of a UV Sphere Object.

Stroke Material Color set in the **Properties Editor, Material Properties**

Figure 9.8

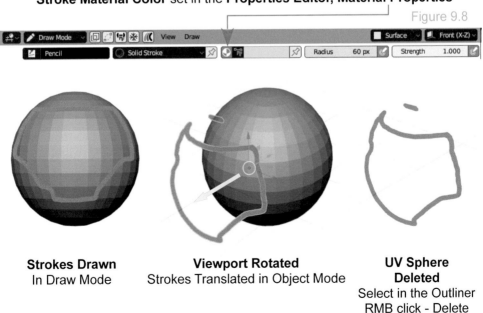

Strokes Drawn
In Draw Mode

Viewport Rotated
Strokes Translated in Object Mode

UV Sphere Deleted
Select in the Outliner
RMB click - Delete

9.3 Coloring Strokes

When the 3D Viewport is placed in Solid Viewport Shading Mode to see the Procedural Object with definition you lose the ability to use the **Color Attribute** option in the **Properties Editor, Active Tool and Workspace Settings**. To color Strokes in Solid Viewport Shading Mode you employ the **Properties Editor, Material Properties**.

Figure 9.9

Properties Editor

Color Attribute   **Material Properties**

Properties Editor, Material Properties

Properties Editor, Active Tool and Workspace Settings

By Drawing Strokes on an Object's surface then deleting the Object you use the Object as a template for creating Strokes using the shape of the Object. The Strokes created can be Edited (modified) and Animated, given Geometry or converted back into a Mesh after Editing.

Warning: Using a 3D Object as a template can produce erratic results.

9.4 3D from 2D

In the Grease Pencil a Model is created by drawing Strokes in a Canvas. A Canvas has been described as being a Three Dimensional Container, therefore, Strokes in the Canvas may be arranged to create a three dimensional shape, which converts to a 3D Object.

Besides arranging Strokes into a shape, individual Strokes may be given **Geometry**. This means the Stroke is given form which displays the Stroke as a Three Dimensional Object. This process may be applied to a single Stroke or multiple Strokes.

Whether arranging Strokes to create an Object or giving a Stroke Geometry, the final result depends on Drawing and arranging the Stroke or Strokes in 3D Space. Controlling and Placing Strokes is described in Chapter 6 but requires further explanation specific to Modeling using the Grease Pencil.

9.5 Modeling from a Stroke

The simplest Model that may be created in the Grease Pencil is to generate a model of a geometric shape from a simple Stroke. The Stroke is Drawn in the 2D Viewport Editor in a Canvas in one of the Layers (see Chapters 2 and 5).

Viewport Header – Draw Mode   Figure 9.10

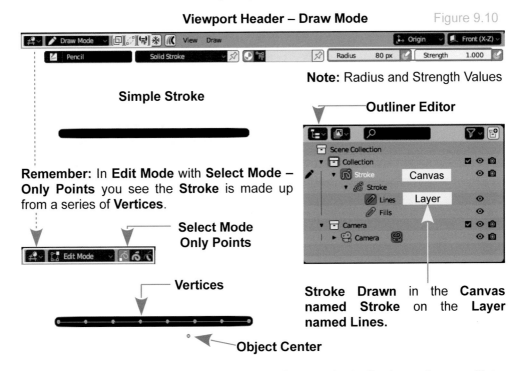

Note: Radius and Strength Values

Simple Stroke

Outliner Editor

Remember: In **Edit Mode** with **Select Mode – Only Points** you see the **Stroke** is made up from a series of **Vertices**.

Canvas

Layer

Select Mode Only Points

Vertices

Stroke Drawn in the **Canvas** named **Stroke** on the **Layer** named **Lines.**

Object Center

Basic Procedure: When creating a Model from a single Stroke or from multiple Strokes, the Strokes are Drawn, then Converted to **Paths**. **Geometry** is created from the Path or applied to the Path. The Path is finally converted to a **Mesh** (Mesh Object). All Strokes Drawn in a Layer in the Canvas are treated as a single Object, therefore, multiple Strokes create one single Object. When **Converted** they create a single **Mesh Model**.

Converting, in this case, means changing from a **Grease Pencil Stroke** to a **Path** or changing from a **Path** to a **Mesh**. A **Path** in Blender is a Curve used to control the shape of a Mesh when Modeling.

Important: When Drawing multiple Strokes to create a Model have all the Strokes in one Layer in the Canvas. To demonstrate the conversion process the Stroke Drawn in Figure 9.10 will be used. Note that this Stroke has been Drawn using the **Line Tool** from the Draw Mode Tool Panel.

Convert to Path

With the Stroke Drawn in the 3D Viewport in **Draw Mode** change to **Object Mode**. The Stroke will be selected as shown by an orange outline. RMB Click in the Viewport and select **Convert to Path**. Alternatively click **Object** in the Viewport Header – **Convert** – **Path**.

At this point you see no change in the 3D Viewport. The Stroke remains selected and displays with the same Vertices when in Edit Mode.

Figure 9.11

Note: The new **Lines** entry in the **Outliner Editor.**

The new entry named **Lines** is the **Path** (Curve).

Click on **Lines** in the **Outliner Editor** to select the **Path** then in the 3D Viewport (Object Mode) use the **Move Tool** (Displays the Move Widget) to drag the Path away from the Stroke Object.

Figure 9.12

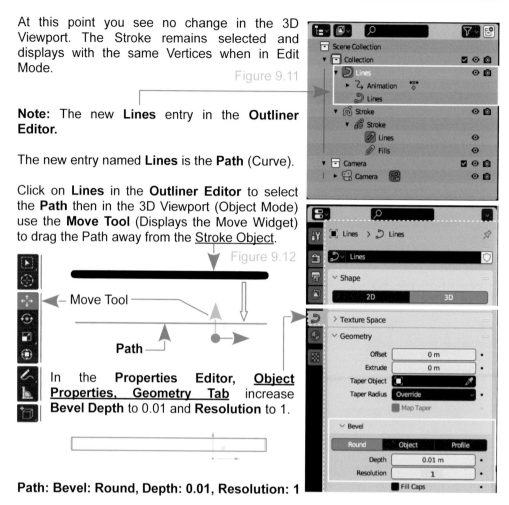

Move Tool

Path

In the **Properties Editor, Object Properties, Geometry Tab** increase **Bevel Depth** to 0.01 and **Resolution** to 1.

Path: Bevel: Round, Depth: 0.01, Resolution: 1

With the **Bevel** values set, change the 3D Viewport to **Solid Viewport Shading Mode** and Rotate the view to see the Geometry applied to the Path.

By adjusting the **Depth** and **Resolution** values you change the shape of the Geometry.

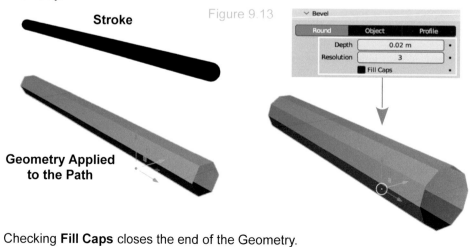

Stroke

Figure 9.13

Geometry Applied
to the Path

Checking **Fill Caps** closes the end of the Geometry.

With **Lines** selected in the **Outliner Editor**, the Viewport display shows Geometry (Bevel Depth and Resolution) created about the Path. By changing the Viewport to Edit Mode you see the **Path at the center of the Geometry** (all Vertices selected).

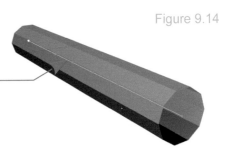

Figure 9.14

Press the **A Key** to deselect the Vertices. **Turn on Proportional Editing**. Press the **C Key** (Circle Select). Scroll MMB to adjust the **Circle of Influence**. Place the circle over the Vertices to be selected and click LMB. Press the **G Key** (Grab). Adjust the new Circle of Influence to select Vertices to be affected. Drag the Mouse to shape the Object.

Figure 9.15   **3D Viewport Header**
Proportional Editing

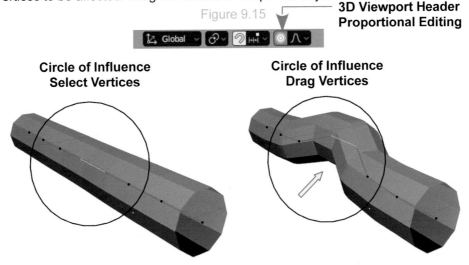

Circle of Influence
Select Vertices

Circle of Influence
Drag Vertices

Convert to Mesh

The final step in creating a Model, using this method, is to convert the Path and its Geometry to a Mesh (Mesh Object). With the Viewport in **Object Mode** and **Lines selected in the Outliner Editor** (Geometry selected in the Viewport) **RMB Click** in the Viewport and select **Convert to Mesh** from the menu.

In **Edit Mode** you see the Mesh Object with its Vertices, Edges and Faces.

You may now select Vertices and refine the shape of the Object.

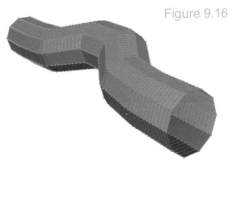

Figure 9.16

Figure 9.17

Tip: In the **Grease Pencil**, pressing the **Z Key** with the Mouse Cursor in the 3D Viewport displays a **Pie Menu** for selecting different **Viewport Display Options**.

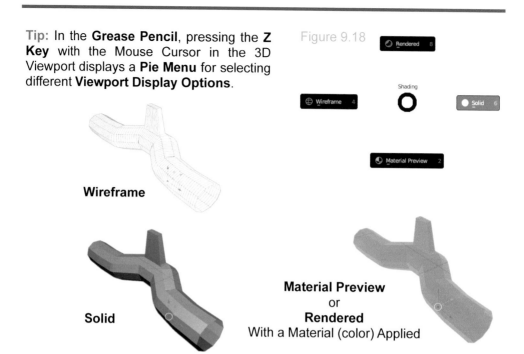

Figure 9.18

Wireframe

Solid

Material Preview
or
Rendered
With a Material (color) Applied

9.6 Combining and Converting Strokes

By Drawing several **Curved Strokes** with the origin at the position of the 3D Cursor, converting to a Path, converting to a Mesh and applying a Material Color a striking simple Model may be created (For the procedure see Section 9.4).

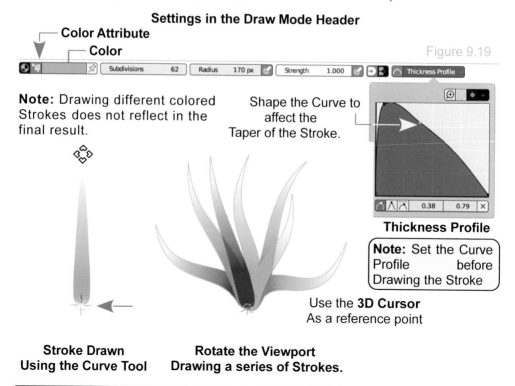

Settings in the Draw Mode Header

Color Attribute

Color

Figure 9.19

Note: Drawing different colored Strokes does not reflect in the final result.

Shape the Curve to affect the
Taper of the Stroke.

Thickness Profile

Note: Set the Curve Profile before Drawing the Stroke

Use the **3D Cursor**
As a reference point

Stroke Drawn
Using the Curve Tool

Rotate the Viewport
Drawing a series of Strokes.

Material Preview Viewport Shading Figure 9.20

Strokes Converted to **Path** – Moved Aside   **Path** Converted to **Mesh**

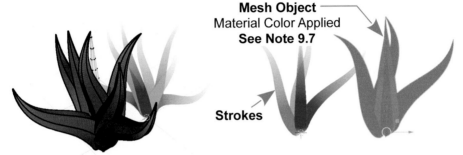

Mesh Object
Material Color Applied
See Note 9.7

Strokes

Solid Viewport Shading   **Rendered Viewport Shading**
(Viewport Rotated)

9.7 Thickness Profile and Color Attribute

When demonstrating **Combining and Converting Strokes** (Section 9.6) different **Color Attribute** settings were used for different Strokes in conjunction with the **Thickness Profile Curve.** The Thickness Profile Curve determines the Taper of the Stroke.

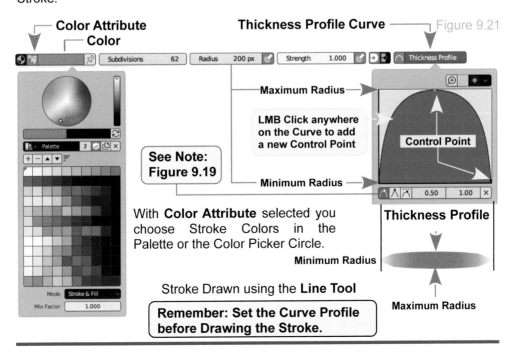

Color Attribute
Color

Thickness Profile Curve ——— Figure 9.21

Subdivisions 62   Radius 200 px   Strength 1.000   Thickness Profile

Maximum Radius—

LMB Click anywhere on the Curve to add a new Control Point

Control Point

See Note: Figure 9.19

Minimum Radius ——

0.50   1.00   ×

With **Color Attribute** selected you choose Stroke Colors in the Palette or the Color Picker Circle.

Thickness Profile

Minimum Radius

Stroke Drawn using the **Line Tool**

Remember: Set the Curve Profile before Drawing the Stroke.

Maximum Radius

Palette 2

+ − ▲ ▼

Mode Stroke & Fill

Mix Factor 1.000

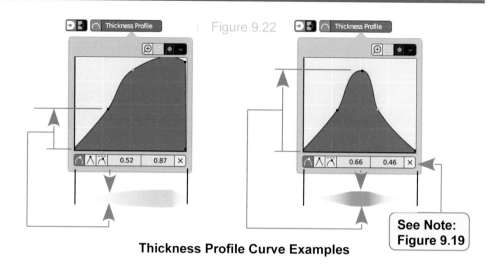

Figure 9.22

Thickness Profile Curve Examples

See Note:
Figure 9.19

9.8 Active Tool and Workspace

Properties Editor

Figure 9.23

Active Tool and Workspace settings ➔

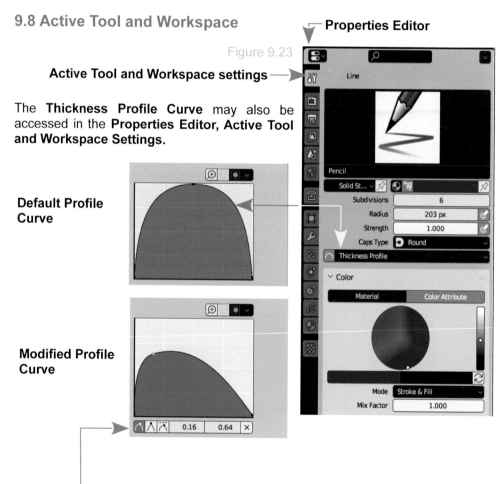

The **Thickness Profile Curve** may also be accessed in the **Properties Editor, Active Tool and Workspace Settings.**

Default Profile Curve

Modified Profile Curve

Note: Values for adjusting the Stroke only display when the default profile Curve has been modified.

9.9 3D Modeling from Strokes

To create a 3D Model you have to consider Drawing separate Strokes in different Views.

Change the 2D Viewport Editor to Front Orthographic View (Press Num Pad 1). The Viewport will display with the icon representing the Camera in the center of the Screen. Go to the Outliner Editor and click the Eye Icon adjacent to Camera to hide the Camera.

To keep orientated when changing perspective (viewing from different angles) it is advantageous to have the grid reference in the Viewport. In the **Viewport Overlays** (See Chapter 6 – 6.2) check **Floor** to display the reference Grid in the Viewport. **Note:** The Grid only displays in Top, Side and Front Views. It does not display in Camera View (Num Pad 0).

To assist in positioning Strokes have the **3D Cursor** active. In the **Viewport Overlays**, check **3D Cursor**. The Cursor will display at the center of the Viewport.

To Draw Strokes relative to the 3D Cursor change **Origin** to **3D Cursor** in the Viewport Header.

Figure 9.24

Origin to 3D Cursor

Drawing relative to the 3D Cursor locates the Stroke on the Plane where the 3D Cursor is located.

Figure 9.25

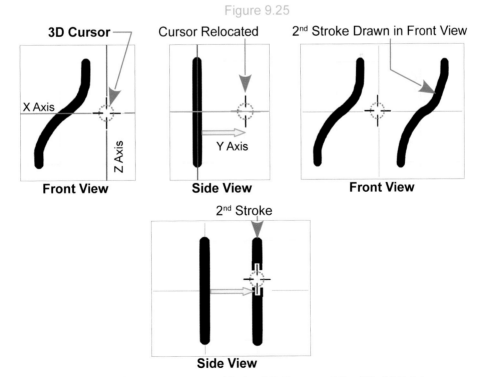

In Front View the 1st Stroke is Drawn with the 3D Cursor at the World Origin.

Another way of explaining **Stroke placement relative to the 3D Cursor** is to look at a 3D View.

Figure 9.26

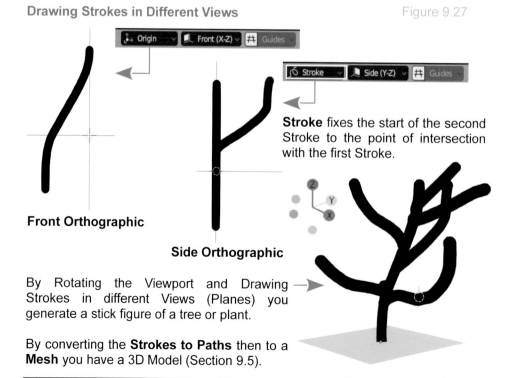

1ˢᵗ Stroke – **Front View on the X-Z Plane**

X Y

Z Z

Side View – Y- Z Plane
3D Cursor relocated

3D Cursor Relocated

Widget

Use the Widget to Rotate the Viewport

Second Stroke Drawn on the X-Z Plane is located on a **Plane at the position of the 3D Cursor.**

Drawing Strokes in Different Views

Figure 9.27

Origin | Front (X-Z) | Guides

Stroke | Side (Y-Z) | Guides

Stroke fixes the start of the second Stroke to the point of intersection with the first Stroke.

Front Orthographic

Side Orthographic

By Rotating the Viewport and Drawing Strokes in different Views (Planes) you generate a stick figure of a tree or plant.

By converting the **Strokes to Paths** then to a **Mesh** you have a 3D Model (Section 9.5).

Animating Strokes

In its simplest form a 2D Computer Animation is a single Stroke appearing to move on the computer Screen. Complex Animations involve numerous Strokes, all of which appear to move, perhaps simultaneously, telling a story or conveying a message.

An Animation takes place during a period of time, therefore, it is said to work on a **Timeline**.

The very basic method of creating an Animation is to draw Strokes representing the shape of an Object in different poses, then display the poses at different **Frames** in a **Timeline**. In Blender's **2D Animation Workspace** the **Dope Sheet Timeline Editor** and the **Timeline Editor** are displayed below the **2D Viewport Editor**. By default the **Dope Sheet Timeline** is fully open but only the **Header** of the **Timeline Editor** is displayed.

Dope Sheet Editor   Figure 10.1

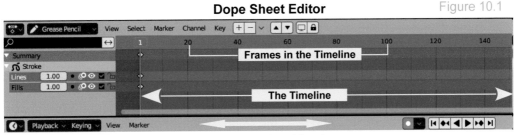

Timeline Editor Header

In the **Timeline**, **Keyframes** are created, recording the position of Strokes at that specific location (the Pose of a Character). The computer can, within limits, automatically create what occurs inbetween the Keyframes (the changes in a Character's Pose).

Properties Editor

10.1 The Bouncing Ball   Figure 10.2

Stroke Animation was briefly demonstrated in the Introduction. To expand on this topic a Character will be created consisting of a single **Circle Stroke** with a **Fill** using **Material Properties.**

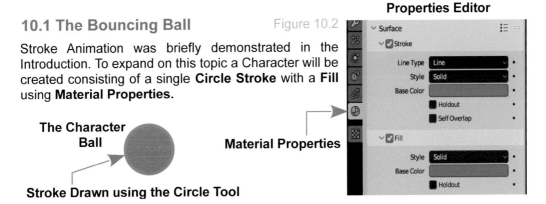

The Character Ball

Material Properties

Stroke Drawn using the Circle Tool

107

The Character is Posed at Keyframes in the Animation Timeline.

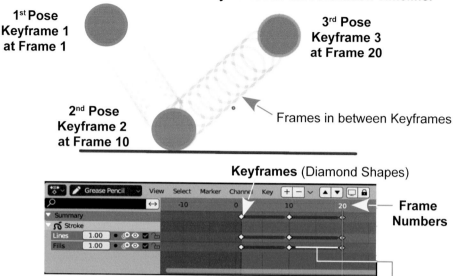

**1st Pose
Keyframe 1
at Frame 1**

**3rd Pose
Keyframe 3
at Frame 20**

**2nd Pose
Keyframe 2
at Frame 10**

Frames in between Keyframes

Keyframes (Diamond Shapes)

**Frame
Numbers**

Dope Sheet Timeline (Segment)   In-between Frames

The position of the Ball is recorded at Keyframe 1, Keyframe 2, and Keyframe 3. The computer works out the **In-between Frames**.

10.2 Dope Sheet and Timeline Editors

The **Dope Sheet** and **Timeline Editors** are where **Keyframes** are set and the length and the speed of an animation sequence is controlled. An Animation Sequence is a segment of animation which will ultimately be combined with other sequences to produce a video file.

The **Dope Sheet** and **Timeline Editors** are displayed in the **2D Animation Workspace** below the 3D Viewport Editor. By default the Dope Sheet Timeline is fully open while the Timeline Editor is minimized. **Note:** It is not necessary to display the Timeline Editor in full, since, at this stage, only the **Play Buttons** in the Header will be used.

Timeline Cursors (blue lines)

Figure 10.4

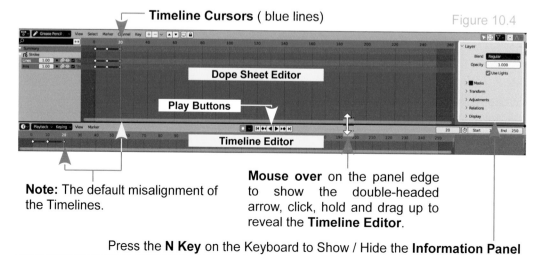

Dope Sheet Editor

Play Buttons

Timeline Editor

Note: The default misalignment of the Timelines.

Mouse over on the panel edge to show the double-headed arrow, click, hold and drag up to reveal the **Timeline Editor**.

Press the **N Key** on the Keyboard to Show / Hide the **Information Panel**

Aligning the Timelines

Figure 10.5

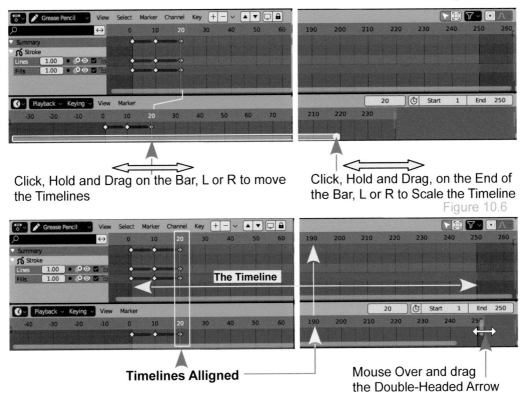

Click, Hold and Drag on the Bar, L or R to move the Timelines

Click, Hold and Drag, on the End of the Bar, L or R to Scale the Timeline

Figure 10.6

Timelines Alligned

Mouse Over and drag the Double-Headed Arrow

Timeline Editor Play Buttons

The **Animation Play Buttons** are located in the center of the Timeline Editor Header (see Figure 10.7).

The Play Buttons control the Play of the Animation much like the controls on any video player.

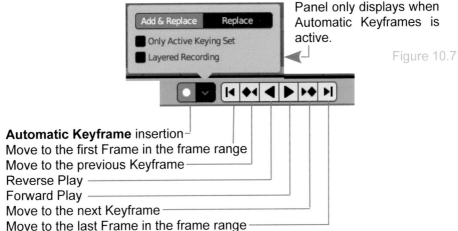

Panel only displays when Automatic Keyframes is active.

Figure 10.7

Automatic Keyframe insertion
Move to the first Frame in the frame range
Move to the previous Keyframe
Reverse Play
Forward Play
Move to the next Keyframe
Move to the last Frame in the frame range

Automatic Keyframe Insertion: With **Auto Keyframe** active (Highlighted blue), Keyframes are automatically inserted in the Timeline when a Frame in the Timeline has been selected and the Character's Pose is changed.

10.3 Animation Basics

To demonstrate the basics of Animation, a Stroke representing a ball will appear to bounce off a second Stroke representing a surface.

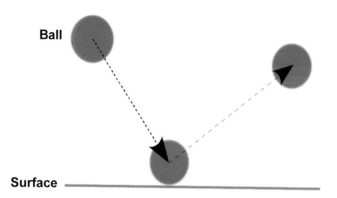

Figure 10.8

To add realism to the Animation the Ball will compress when it strikes the Surface then reshape before bouncing up. To achieve this realism each stage of the action is considered a Pose for which Keyframes are entered in the Timeline.

10.4 Animation Action

Consider the chain of events occurring in the Animation.

The Ball at the initial position   KF 1.
The Ball impacts the surface   KF 2.
The Ball after bouncing   KF 5.

Inbetween KF 2 and KF 5 the Ball:

Compresses on impact   KF 3.
Bounces and resumes shape   KF 4.

Figure 10.9

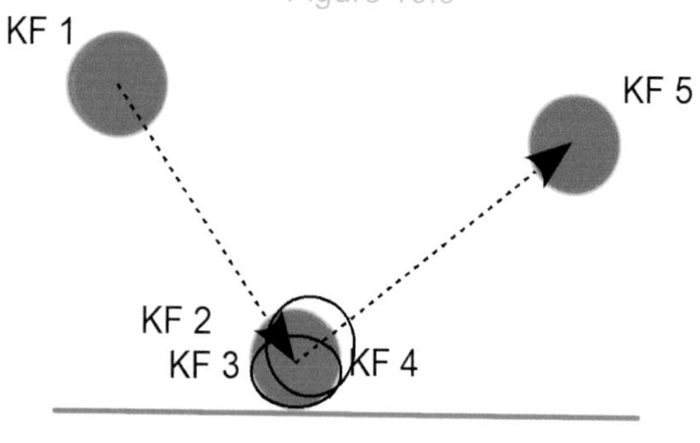

The Animation will take place during 30 Frames. At the default Frame Rate of 24 Frames per Second this will take place in 1.25 Seconds.

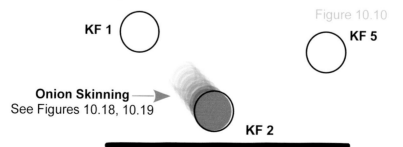

Figure 10.10

When setting up the Animation, KF1, KF2 and KF5 are inserted at Frames 1, 15 and 30 then the detail of compression and reshaping is added afterwards.

10.5 Keyframing and Framing

Note: Keyframes may be inserted manually by positioning the Timeline Cursor at a Frame in the Animation Timeline, selecting the Stroke (Ball) in Edit Mode and positioning (Posing) in the Scene then pressing the **I Key** on the Keyboard and selecting **Insert Keyframe** in the menu that displays.

With **Automatic Keying** activated in the Timeline Editor Header, Keyframes are inserted in the Timeline when the Timeline Cursor is located at a Frame and the Stroke (Ball) is relocated in the 3D Viewport Editor.

The Keying Procedure for the Bouncing Ball

Have the Ball selected in Edit Mode positioned in the air above the Surface Stroke.

Position the Dope Sheet Editor, Timeline Cursor at Frame 1.

With Automatic Keyframing active (highlighted blue) in the Timeline Editor Header a Keyframe is inserted in the Dope Sheet Timeline at Frame 1.

Figure 10.11

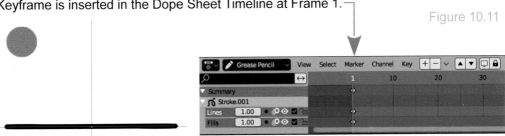

Position the Timeline Cursor at Frame 15. With the Ball selected in Edit Mode (G key Grab) and position the ball on the Plane. A Keyframe is inserted at Frame 15.

Figure 10.12

Position the Timeline Cursor at Frame 30 and reposition the Ball in the air.   Figure 10.13
A keyframe is inserted at Frame 30

Note: Playing the Animation at this stage will see the Ball remain stationary as the Timeline Cursor traverses the Timeline. The Ball will then jump to the second position at the surface of the Plane when the Timeline Cursor reaches Frame 15. The Ball stays at position 2 until the Timeline Cursor reaches Frame 30.

To create a smooth motion between Keyframes the in-between Frames will be created by Interpolation. Before Interpolating consider the following.

When a Ball bounces off a surface it deforms (Squishes) when it strikes the surface then reforms as it rises. To add realism to the Animation incorporate this deformation.

Locate the Timeline Cursor at Frame 15. The Ball moves to position 2 on the surface of the Plane.

Figure 10.14

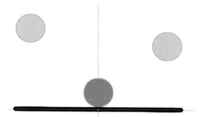

In the **Timeline Editor Header**, Mouse Over on the Frame Number and **click the arrow** to advance to Frame 17.

With the ball selected in Edit Mode Scale down on the Z Axis (S Key + Z key) squishing the Ball then using the Transform Widget move the squished Ball down to the surface of the Plane.

A Keyframe is inserted at Frame 17. Figure 10.15

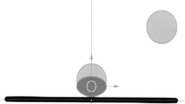
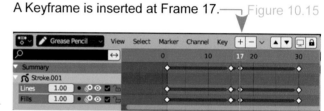

Move the Timeline Cursor to Frame 19. Reshape the Ball and reposition slightly above the squish.

A Keyframe is inserted at Frame 19. Figure 10.16

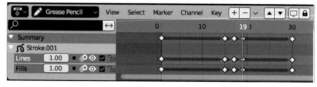

To Interpolate the **In-between Frames** creating a smooth Animation, position the Timeline Cursor between each set of Keyframes (between F1 and F15, between F15 and F17 etc.). With the Timeline Cursor in position, click Grease Pencil in the 3D Viewport Editor Header and select **Interpolate Sequence to produce Inbetween Keys.**

Figure 10.17

Repeat between each set of Keyframes.

With Frames Interpolated between the Keyframes the Animation will play with a smooth motion. However, the motion starts at Frame 1 and stops at Frame 30. This is the Frame Range created. The Timeline Cursor continues to move in the Timeline after Frame 30 until it reaches Frame 250. This is the default length of the Animation. When the Cursor reaches Frame 250 the Animation starts again at Frame 1 and replays (see Section 10.7).

10.6 Onion Skinning

The shadows of the Ball seen in the preceding diagrams are called **Onion Skins** which show where the Stroke (Ball) was located at a preceding Frame in the Animation.

Onion Skinning for a Stroke is controlled in the **Properties Editor, Object data Properties, Onioning Skinning Tab** for the selected Stroke.

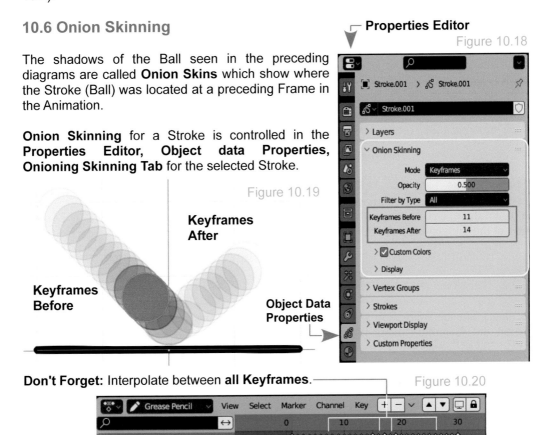

Figure 10.19

Figure 10.18

Properties Editor

Keyframes After

Keyframes Before

Object Data Properties

Don't Forget: Interpolate between **all Keyframes.**　　Figure 10.20

10.7 Animation Time

Animation settings for controling an Animation are located in the **Dope Sheet Editor, Animation Timeline** (Figure 10.21) and in the **Properties Editor, Output Properties, Format Tab and Frame Range Tab** (Figure 10.22).

Dope Sheet Editor - Animation Timeline　　　　　　　　Figure 10.21

Start Frame 1　　**Dope Sheet Editor**　　**End Frame 250**

Timeline Editor Header ➤

The Animation Start Frame, End Frame are set in the Dope Sheet Editor. Setting the End Frame determines the Animation Length.

Properties Editor - Output Properties

Format Tab: Resolution and Aspect are settings which determine Render Properties.

Output Properties→

Frame Rate: The speed of the Animation playback. 24 Frames Per Second is the default value.

1.25 seconds x 24 Frames per second = 30 Frames

Animation Time ◢

Frame Range Tab: Set the Start Frame and End Frame of the Animation thus determining the length of Animation. This is replicating the settings at the end of the Timeline Editor Header (Figure 10.23).

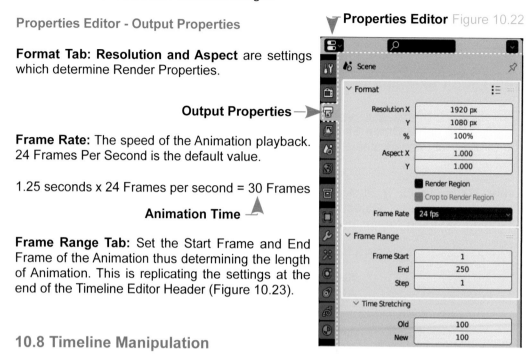

▼**Properties Editor** Figure 10.22

10.8 Timeline Manipulation

At this point the Animation takes place, starting at Frame 1 and ending at Frame 30. When the Animation plays the Ball descends, bounces and stops at Frame 30. The Dope Sheet Timeline Cursor continues to move to Frame 250 then jumps back to Frame 1 and replays over.

In the Timeline Editor Header change the **End** Frame to 30 (lower RHS of the Screen).

Figure 10.23

Replaying the animation sees the Ball bounce over and over and over but the Ball relocates from its position at Frame 30 back to its position at Frame 1. To make a continuous movement and set up a perpetual motion animation consider the following.

10.9 Perpetual Motion

Figure 10.24

A Ball inside a Circle

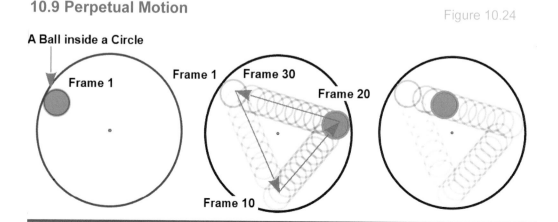

To create a Perpetual Motion simulation see the following settings.

Note: The Ball and the Circle have been Drawn in separate Canvases created in the **Outliner Editor** (Figure 10.25).

The Ball has been positioned inside the Circle at Frames 1, 10, 20 and 30 of the Animation creating Keyframes. Interpolation between Keyframes has been performed.

The End Frame for the Animation has been set at Frame 30 which creates the illusion of Perpetual Motion as the Animation plays over and over.

Figure 10.25

Dope Sheet Timeline   Figure 10.26

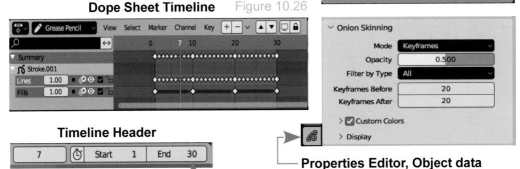

Timeline Header

End Frame

Properties Editor, Object data Properties for the **Ball.**

10.10 The Walk Cycle and Animation

The **Walk Cycle** (Figure 10.27) shows a series of images depicting a figure walking. If each image were displayed in quick succession you would see an animation of the figure walking. This method is called **Time Laps Animation** and requires that each pose is drawn separately. For the Image see:

https://webneel.com/daily/1-walk-cycle?size=_original

In the Grease Pencil you can trace Strokes from one of the pose images (Chapter 8).

Figure 10.27

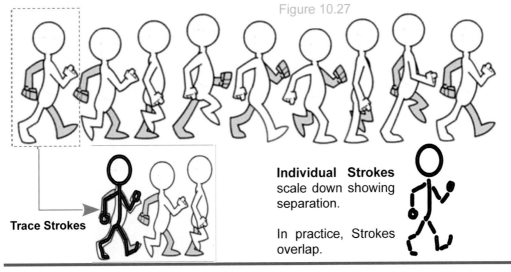

Trace Strokes

Individual Strokes scale down showing separation.

In practice, Strokes overlap.

Tracing individual Strokes constructs the components of the character (arms, legs etc.) The Strokes may then be posed in Edit Mode at different Frames to create an animation.

If you would like to try this method, it is suggested you trace a simple stick figure which will show the technique before delving into too much detail.

Even with a Stick Figure you have to consider how you draw the individual Strokes forming the Character. You should trace individual Strokes which will allow you to select and reposition the components of the Character at different Frames in the Animation.

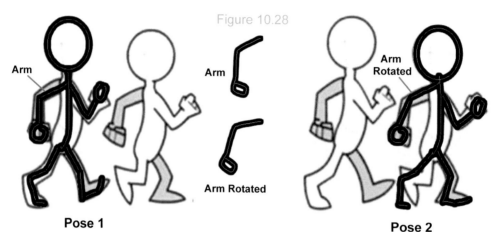

Figure 10.28

Pose 1 **Pose 2**

Strokes repositioned (Posed) at the second **Keyframe** in the Animation Timeline.

Keyframes in the Animation Timeline determine how fast your Character walks. A little arithmetic is required.

Assuming 2 seconds to traverse the Screen. The Walk Cycle has 9 Poses, therefore, 9 Keyframes are required. The default Frame playback rate is 24 FPS. 2 seconds x 24 FPS = 48 Frames. 9 Poses, therefore, 8 Frame Groups. 48 / 8 = 6 Frames in a group = Keyframe every 6th Frame, i.e. F1, F6,F12, F18, etc.

10.11 Keyframes and Posing

Drawing Strokes (Tracing in Draw Mode) at the first Pose, with the Dope Sheet Timeline Cursor at Frame 1, generates the first Keyframe of an Animation when Auto Keying is activated.

Move the Timeline Cursor to frame 6.

Remember: 6 Frames in a Group.

In **Edit Mode** with all the Strokes selected, drag over to **Pose 2.**

All Strokes Selected
(Press A Key)

Remember: Which Use the Move Tool to
Select Mode Translate.

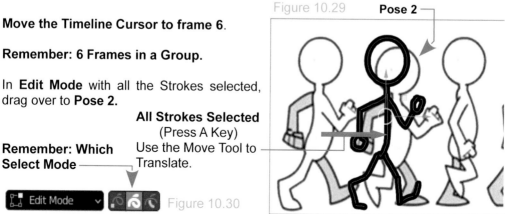

Figure 10.29   **Pose 2**

Edit Mode   Figure 10.30

With the Strokes positioned at Pose 2 individually select each Stroke and Translate (G Key), Rotate (R Key) to align with Pose 2.

Figure 10.31

Aligning the Strokes with Pose 2, with the Timeline Cursor at Frame 6 generates the second Keyframe.

Individual Stroke (upper leg)
Rotated (R Key) Repositioned
(G Key)

From this point on you repeat the procedure at each Pose, generating **Keyframes** every 6th Frame i.e. F1, F6, F12, F18, etc. (9 Keyframes Total).

Figure 10.32

Finally perform **Interpolation Sequence** operations (Figure 10.17) between each Keyframe generating the in-between Frames in the Animation.

Figure 10.33

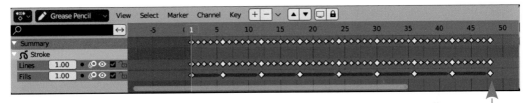

Don't forget to set the Animation End frame to 48.

With the Animation frames generated, position the Timeline Cursor at Frame 1 and play the Animation to see the Stick Figure walk across the Screen. You can hide the Animation Sequence Reference Image by clicking the Eye Icon in the Outliner Editor adjacent to Empty (the Canvas named Empty).

Reference Image

Onion Skinning

Figure 10.34

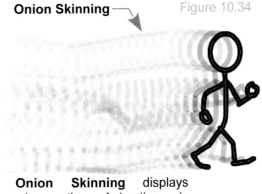

Onion Skinning displays when the Animation is paused.

The foregoing method of Animating Strokes may be suitable for simple Animations but would constitute a very tedious procedure when a detailed Character is Animated.

See Chapters 11 and 12 for further details.

Figure 10.35

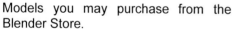
Models you may purchase from the Blender Store.

10.12 Armatures for Posing

Individually positioning Strokes to generate Keyframes will be fine when using a simple character such as the Stick Figure. As you can imagine, this would be a tedious process with a character comprising numerous Strokes required to create the Characters shown in Figure 10.35. In this case, **Armatures** would be employed to simplify the operation.

An **Armature** is a **Non-renderable Object**, meaning it does not Render, therefore, it is not displayed in an Image or a Frame in an Animation.

The Procedure

The basic philosophy of Posing a Character using Armatures is to position the Armature in proximity to Strokes which form a component of the Character. For example, an Arm of the Character, then associate (Link / Parent) the Armature to the Strokes such that when the Armature is moved the Strokes follow. This is performed at different Frames in the Animation Timeline where Keyframes are generated (see Chapter 11).

11

Animating a Character

Character animation is, perhaps, the ultimate goal in using the Grease Pencil 2D Animation Workspace. The preceding chapters have introduced the program's interface and the tools for drawing which enable you to construct a Scene and perform simple Animation.

Chapter 10 has demonstrated how Strokes may be Animated to represent a Character walking in a Scene. It is obvious that, even with the simple stick figure, it is a tedious process to manipulate Strokes from one Pose to the next and the task is daunting when the number of different poses is taken into consideration. There is another way!

Trace each Pose creating Keyframes. When Interpolation is applied, Blender calculates the difference between the shape of the Stroke at one Keyframe and the next and fills in the In-between Frames (Poses).

11.1 Basic Concept

Using the Walk Cycle Image Trace a Stroke at Frame 1. Trace a Stroke at Frame 20. Interpolate between Frame 1 and Frame 20. The Stroke is transposed in the Animation.

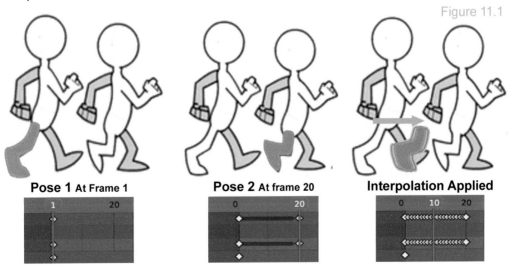

Figure 11.1

Pose 1 At Frame 1   Pose 2 At frame 20   Interpolation Applied

Figure 11.1 shows when the Animation is played, after Interpolation is applied, the Stroke Traced at Pose 1 (Frame 1) is Transposed to Pose 2 (Frame 20).

11.2 Walk Cycle Reference Image

The Walk Cycle Reference Image depicts different Poses of a Character walking. When drawing a series of Poses for any movement, the more Poses the better. More Poses will mean a more even movement in the Animation when each Pose is displayed in succession. Bear in mind that drawing a Pose takes time, therefore, you have to strike a balance between drawing time and the quality of the animation.

Walk Cycle Reference Image Figure 11.2

In the Reference Image, observe that there are 9 Poses. Pose 1 is identical to Pose 9, Pose 5 shows arms and legs opposite to Pose 1 and 9, Pose 2 arms and legs are opposite to Pose 6, Pose 3 arms and legs are opposite to Pose 7, and Pose 4 is an opposite to Pose 8.

To enter the Reference Image in the 3D Viewport change the Viewport to **Object Mode** (see Chapter 8 – Section 8.2).

When the Walk Cycle is entered in the 3D Viewport Editor as a Reference Image it is treated as a non-renderable Object in the Scene. This means that it does not become part of the final Animation. When the Image is entered it is in Object Mode. In Object Mode you may Scale (S Key drag the Mouse), Rotate (R Key drag the Mouse) and translate (G Key drag the Mouse) or use Tools, to suit the view.

Figure 11.3

Outliner Editor

Remember: When a Reference Image is entered in the 3D Viewport it is entered as an Empty Object as seen in the Outliner Editor.

Figure 11.4

The Image entered in the following examples is named Screen-Hunter2919.tif. By searching the Internet you will find literally hundreds of examples.

When a Reference Image is added it is entered in the Datablock name **Empty** which refers to an **Empty Object** and by default is the selected Object.

11.3 Tracing Strokes

Before you can draw Strokes you have to select the **Datablock** named **Stroke** in the Outliner Editor. **Stroke** is the Canvas containing two Layers named Lines and Fills with the default Lines Layer selected. You will, therefore, Trace Strokes in the Lines Layer.

Have **Automatic Keyframing** activated (highlighted) in the **Timeline Editor Header**.

For this demonstration Strokes are Drawn with the 3D Viewport in Camera Perspective View. Zoom in on the Viewport to fill the view with the Reference Image. Alternately, with the Viewport in Object Mode you may select Empty (the Image) in the Outliner Editor then Scale the Image in the 3D Viewport.

In either case have the Reference Image fill the Screen.

Select **Stroke** in the Outliner Editor and change the 3D Viewport to Draw Mode.

Set the Stroke parameters in the **3D Viewport Header**. Figure 11.5

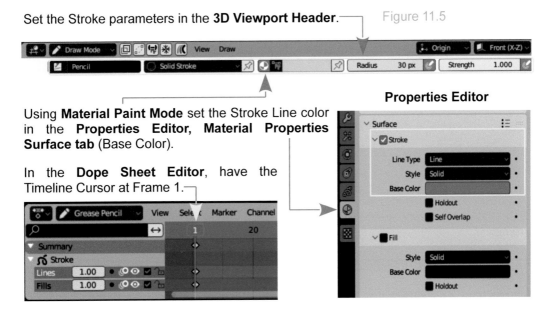

Properties Editor

Using **Material Paint Mode** set the Stroke Line color in the **Properties Editor, Material Properties Surface tab** (Base Color).

In the **Dope Sheet Editor**, have the Timeline Cursor at Frame 1.

Trace Strokes over the first Pose in the Walk Cycle Reference Image.

Pose 1 Figure 11.6

Tracing Strokes with **Automatic Keyframing** active enters a Keyframe in the Dope Sheet Timeline Editor.

Keyframes are entered in the Dope Sheet Timeline for Pose 1 at Frame 1.

Trace Strokes for Poses 2 to 8 at every Tenth Frame in the Timeline. Drawing at every Tenth Frame is merely for convenience and clarity during the Drawing process. The spacing of Keyframes will be adjusted later. Pose 9 is not required since it is identical to Pose 1.

Move the Timeline Cursor to Frame Ten and Trace Strokes over Pose 2. Repeat the Tracing process for each Pose in the reference Image except Pose 9.

Keyframe for Pose 1   Figure 11.7   **Keyframe for Pose 8**

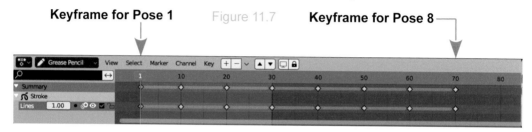

If **Interpolation** were to be applied between Keyframes and the Animation played you would be disappointed to see some rather chaotic results.

Figure 11.8

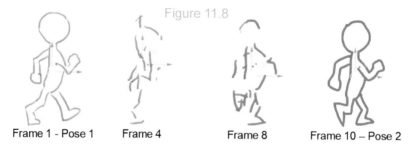

Frame 1 - Pose 1   Frame 4   Frame 8   Frame 10 – Pose 2

With anything but very simple Strokes the system struggles to calculate the in-between Frames.

11.4 Scaling and Positioning Keyframes

Scaling and positioning the Keyframes in the Timeline will give a better result by smoothing the Animation.

With the Mouse Cursor in the Dope Sheet Timeline Editor press the **A Key** to select all the Keyframes (white diamonds turn yellow – selected).

Figure 11.9

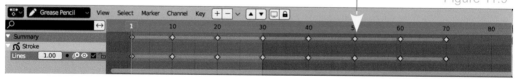

With the Timeline Cursor at Frame 1 (all Keyframes selected) and the **Mouse Cursor in the Timeline Editor**, press the **S Key** and drag the Mouse to the left. The selected group of Keyframes will contract (scale down) relative to the position of the Timeline Cursor.

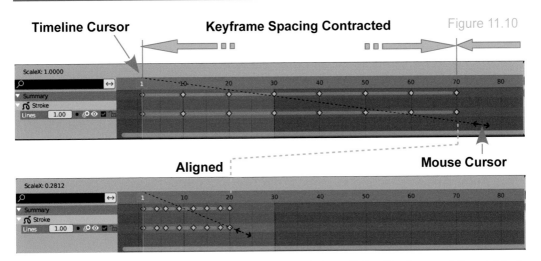

Timeline Cursor **Keyframe Spacing Contracted** Figure 11.10

Aligned **Mouse Cursor**

Scale down by dragging the Mouse Cursor to the left until the Keyframe at the right of the group is aligned with Frame 20.

Playing the Animation at this point will see the eight Poses flash across the Screen while the Timeline Cursor moves from Frame 1 to Frame 20. The transition between Poses is much smoother but it is over in 20 Frames (0.833 sec) with the Timeline Cursor continuing on to Frame 250 before repeating.

To control the Walk Cycle employ a **Modifier**.

11.5 The Time Offset Modifier

Properties Editor

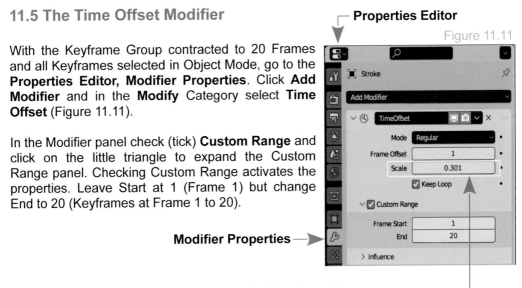

Figure 11.11

With the Keyframe Group contracted to 20 Frames and all Keyframes selected in Object Mode, go to the **Properties Editor, Modifier Properties**. Click **Add Modifier** and in the **Modify** Category select **Time Offset** (Figure 11.11).

In the Modifier panel check (tick) **Custom Range** and click on the little triangle to expand the Custom Range panel. Checking Custom Range activates the properties. Leave Start at 1 (Frame 1) but change End to 20 (Keyframes at Frame 1 to 20).

Modifier Properties ➞

Adjust the **Scale** value to control the speed of the Animation.

Reducing the Scale value to 0.301 or 0.201 reduces the speed of the Animation but the result is a jerky walk by the Character.

An alternative method is to Transpose the Strokes at each Frame such that the Character walks from one Pose to the next instead of traversing the Screen.

11.6 Transposing Strokes

Add a Walk Cycle Reference Image in the Scene and as previously described (see Section 11.2) trace Strokes over each Pose (1 to 8) with the Dope Sheet Timeline Cursor at different Frames.

Note: Before Tracing, select the default Keyframe in the Dope Sheet Timeline and delete. With the default Keyframe left in situ, the first Strokes Traced will be entered at Frame 2.

Have **Automatic Keyframing** engaged in the **Timeline Editor Header**.   Figure 11.12

Pose 1 at Frame 1   Figure 11.13

Pose 3 at Frame 40   Figure 11.14   **Not Required**

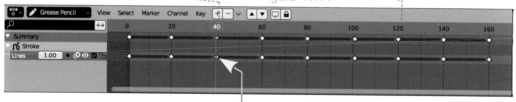

As Strokes are Drawn at each Pose, Keyframes are inserted in the Timeline. Playing the Animation at this point will see the Strokes jump from one Pose to the next as each Frame is reached.

With the Reference Image spanning the Screen the Character appears to move across the Screen in a series of Poses. The Poses constitute only one step and, therefore, need to be consolidated and duplicated to produce a more realistic walk.

Place the Timeline Cursor at the second Keyframe selecting Pose 2. In Figure 11.14 this is at Frame 20. Place the 3D Viewport in Edit Mode and press the A key to select all the Strokes making up Pose 2.

Using the **Move Tool from the Tool Panel** move the Strokes to the left aligning the left leg heal of Pose 2 with the left leg heal of Pose 1.

Note: The left foot of the Character is in contact with the surface and, therefore, stationary relative to the surface at each Pose.

Repeat the Stroke positioning procedure for each Pose aligning whichever limb is in contact with the surface form the previous Pose. You can see this with **Onion Skinning** activated. **Tip:** With Stroke selected, in the **Data Properties, Onion Skinning Tab**, have Keyframes Before = 1 and Keyframes After = 0.

Figure 11.15

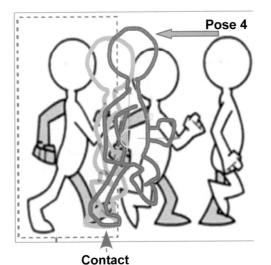

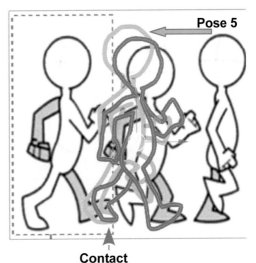

With the Strokes repositioned, playing the Animation will see the Pose change as the Timeline Cursor passes each Frame to Frame 160 then repeats. Figure 11.16

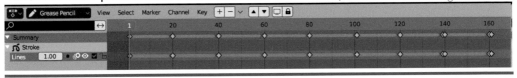

With the Timeline shown in Figure 11.14 spanning 160 Frames the single Walk Cycle, one step forward takes 6.66 seconds which is a slow motion effect. The Timeline requires consolidation. With the Mouse Cursor in the Timeline press the A Key to select all Keyframes.

Keep the **Mouse Cursor** in the Timeline, press the S Key (Scale) and drag to the left compressing the Keyframes to 30 Frames (Figure 11.17).

Make sure the **Timeline Cursor** is at Frame 1.

Figure 11.17

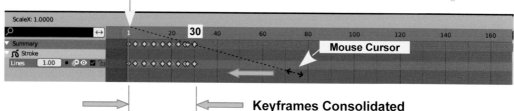

Keyframes Consolidated

In the Timeline Editor Header set the Animation End Frame to **30** which has the Animation play over and over in 30 Frames.

To have the Character walk across the Screen a secondary Animation will be created. Remember, the Stroke Datablock in the Outliner Editor is a Canvas. Blender considers the Canvas to be an Object, therefore, the Canvas (Object) can be Parented to Follow a Path which is a special type of Curve having an Animation Sequence associated.

Place the 3D Viewport in Object mode. You may cancel the display of the Reference Image by clicking the Eye Icon adjacent to Empty (the Image) in the Outliner Editor.

In the **3D Viewport Editor, Header**, click **Add - Curve** and select **Path**.

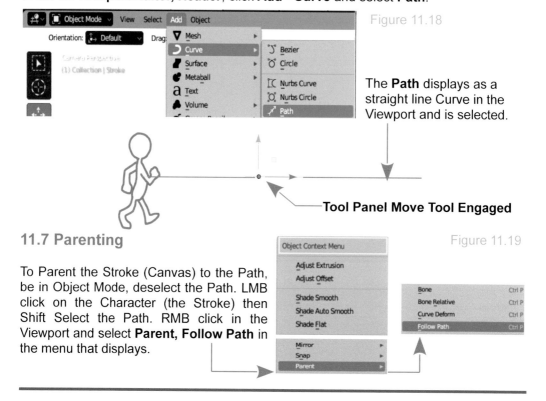

Figure 11.18

The **Path** displays as a straight line Curve in the Viewport and is selected.

Tool Panel Move Tool Engaged

11.7 Parenting

Figure 11.19

To Parent the Stroke (Canvas) to the Path, be in Object Mode, deselect the Path. LMB click on the Character (the Stroke) then Shift Select the Path. RMB click in the Viewport and select **Parent, Follow Path** in the menu that displays.

Playing the Animation at this point sees the Character walk from left to right in the Screen following the Move Tool on the Path. The Animation repeats at Frame 30 since this is the End Frame set in the Timeline Editor. The Keyframes for the Character are spread over 30 Frames.

Figure 11.20

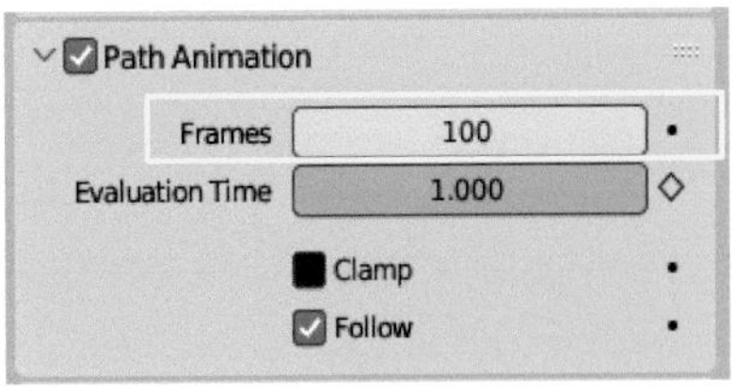

By selecting the Path, in the **Properties Editor, Object Data Properties, Path Animation Tab** for the Path you see the Path length in Frames is 100.

To have the Character walk for the full length of the Path, set the End Frame in the Timeline Editor at 90 (3×30 Frames for the Character Animation).

Figure 11.21

Note: When the Character is Parented to the Path the Canvas (Stroke) is listed in the Outliner Editor under **Nurbs Path**.

Change the number of Frames in the Path Animation Tab to 90.

Select the Character in the 3D Viewport then in the Dope Sheet Timeline (All Keyframes selected) press Shift + D Key (Duplicate) and drag to the right positioning the first frame of the **duplication at Frame 31**.

Figure 11.22

Repeat the duplication.

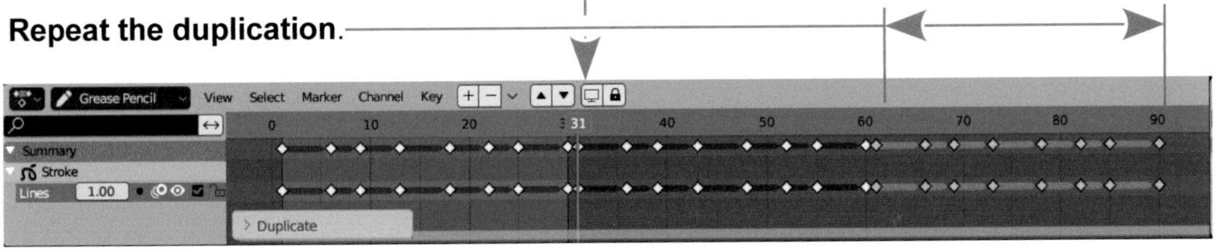

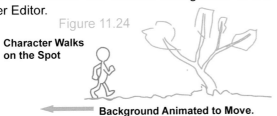

Play the Animation to see the Character walk across the Screen.

11.8 Alternative Procedure

Outliner Editor

Figure 11.23

Instead of duplicating Keyframes, have the Character marking time as the Animation plays. You can create the illusion that the Character walks in the Scene by animating a Background to traverse the Scene opposite to the Walk Cycle.

Figure 11.24 shows a simple Background depicting a ground plane and a tree with all Strokes on the Layer named Lines under the Canvas Background in the Outliner Editor.

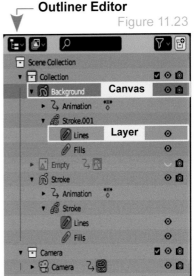

Figure 11.24

Character Walks on the Spot

Background Animated to Move.

Armatures for Posing

Individually positioning Strokes to generate Keyframes will be fine when using a simple character such as the Stick Figure. As you can imagine, this would be a tedious process with a character comprising numerous Strokes. Tracing from a reference image is also a lengthy operation. In this case, **Armatures** are employed to simplify the procedure.

An **Armature** is a **Non-renderable Object**, meaning it does not Render, therefore, is not displayed in an Image or a Frame in an Animation.

12.1 The Armature Object

To add an Armature Object in the 3D Viewport Editor, be in **Object Mode** and click **Add** in the Header. Select **Armature** in the menu that displays.

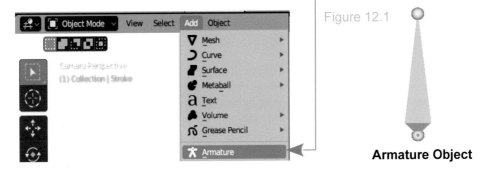

Figure 12.1

Armature Object

In **Object Mode** the Armature Object may be Translated, Rotated and Scaled.

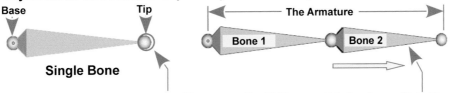

In **Edit Mode** you may <u>select the Tip</u>, press the **E Key** and **Extrude** multiple **Bones**.

Figure 12.2

The Base of the Second Bone is conjoined to the Tip of the First Bone. In Object Mode, Rotating, Translating or Scaling either Bone, affects both Bones.

Note: The **Armature** is enterd in the **Outliner Editor** as a new Datablock.

In **Edit Mode** you may select either Bone and Rotate, Translate or Scale. **The Bones remain conjoined.**

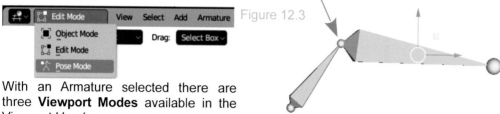

Figure 12.3

With an Armature selected there are three **Viewport Modes** available in the Viewport Header.

In **Pose Mode** you may select either Bone (blue outline).

Rotating or Translating the first Bone affects both Bones.

Rotating the second Bone only affects the second Bone.

Figure 12.4

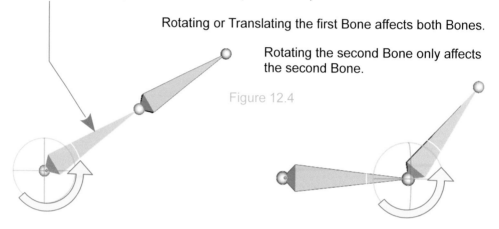

Properties Editor

12.2 Armature Display

Figure 12.5

Armatures can be displayed in the Viewport in five display types by selecting the options in the, **Object Data Properties, Viewport Display Tab**. Have an Armature entered in the Viewport and selected.

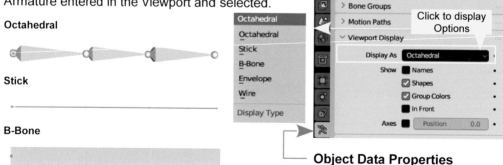

Octahedral

Stick

B-Bone

Envelope

Wire

Object Data Properties

12.3 Using Armatures

Armatures are used to Pose Strokes which have been drawn in the 3D Viewport Editor. Posing a Stroke in the 3D Viewport with the Dope Sheet Editor Cursor positioned at a Frame in the Timeline creates a Keyframe. An Armature is used to alter the Pose of the Stroke at different Frames, creating Keyframes for the Animation in the Timeline.

The following operation will demonstrate the basic procedure.

Drawing Strokes

When Drawing or Tracing Strokes they should encapsulate a component of the character being Animated. Figure 12.6 shows a Stroke encapsulating the Character's right arm. Separate Strokes would be Drawn for the head, left arm, body, right leg and left leg.

Figure 12.6

In Object Mode, add an Armature. In Edit Mode, position the Armature inside the Stroke, extrude a second Bone, Rotate and position relative to the Stroke.

The Bone Armature (two bones) will be Parented to the Stroke such that when the Armature is Posed the Stroke follows the Armature.

Note: Strokes are Drawn with the 3D Viewport in Draw Mode. Strokes are Drawn in the default Canvas in the Lines Layer. Using a Reference Image and Tracing Strokes will have entered a new Datablock in the Outliner Editor for the Reference Image.

In following the procedure you should make note of the changes to the Outliner Editor at each stage of the operation.

Figure 12.7

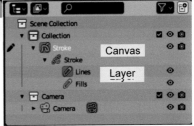

Default Layer Layer: Lines

Figure 12.7 shows the default Outliner Editor before any Strokes are Drawn and before a Reference Image has been added. Strokes drawn in the 3D Viewport will be Drawn in the Canvas named Stroke in the Lines Layer. **Lines** is the selected Layer as seen in the upper RH of the 3D Viewport.

Reference Image for tracing added in the 3D Viewport (Object Mode)

3D Viewport – Object Mode Figure 12.8 **Outliner editor**

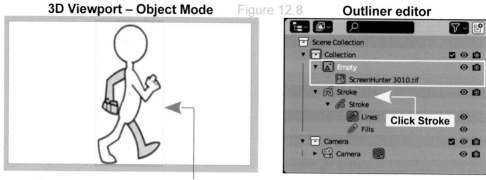

Image – ScreenHunter 3010.tif

The Image ScreenHunter 3010.tif is a Screen Capture of the first Pose in the Walk Cycle.

With the Reference Image in the 3D Viewport (Object Mode), **click on Stroke** in the **Outliner Editor** then change the 3D Viewport to **Draw Mode**. You must click Stroke before you can change to draw Mode.

Draw the Stroke for the Right Arm. Figure 12.9

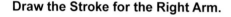

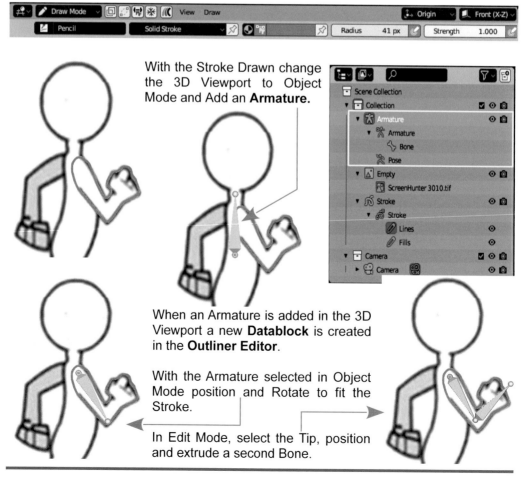

With the Stroke Drawn change the 3D Viewport to Object Mode and Add an **Armature.**

When an Armature is added in the 3D Viewport a new **Datablock** is created in the **Outliner Editor**.

With the Armature selected in Object Mode position and Rotate to fit the Stroke.

In Edit Mode, select the Tip, position and extrude a second Bone.

132

12.4 Parenting

To have the Armature affect the Stroke (Pose the Stroke) the Armature has to be Parented to the Stroke.

In the 3D Viewport, **in Object Mode**, select the Stroke then Shift select the Armature. **Press Ctrl + P** and select **With Automatic Weights** in the menu that displays.

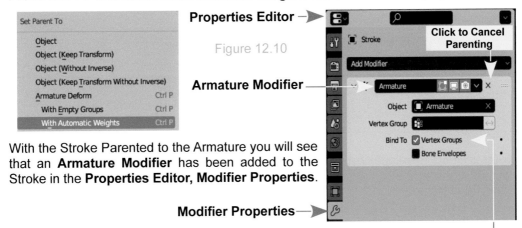

Properties Editor →

Figure 12.10

Armature Modifier ──

With the Stroke Parented to the Armature you will see that an **Armature Modifier** has been added to the Stroke in the **Properties Editor, Modifier Properties**.

Modifier Properties →

Note: Should you wish to cancel the Parenting click the cross in the Modifier Panel.

Note Also: The **Bind To** entry in the Modifier Panel. Bind To ☑ Vertex Groups

Bind To Vertex Groups means that the Armature is Parented to the Stroke by the association of the Armature to the **Vertices of the Stroke**.

Vertices──→

To demonstrate this association select the Armature and have 3D Viewport in **Pose Mode**.

For clarity you may hide the display of the Reference Image by clicking the **Eye Icon** adjacent to **Empty** (the Image) in the **Outliner Editor**.

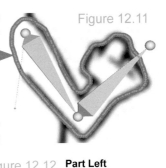

Figure 12.11

Figure 12.12 **Part Left Behind**

In **Pose Mode** select the second Bone in the Armature and Rotate clockwise to see the Stroke deform as the Rotation occurs, **BUT** you will observe that **part of the Stroke** is left behind as the Armature is Rotated.

This occurs since an Armature has a **Field of Influence** and in this case part of the Stroke falls outside the Field. To see the Field of Influence change the Armature Display to **Display as Envelope** (see Section 12.2). Select a Bone.

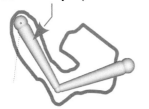

In the **Properties Editor, World Properties** change the color of the Scene background. ──────→

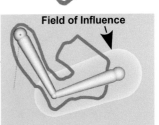

Field of Influence

Figure 12.13
Second Bone selected in **Pose Mode.**

To adjust the Field of Influence have the Armature Bone (second Bone) selected in Pose Mode, before Rotating the Bone, then in the **Properties Editor, Bone Properties, Deform Tab**, increase the **Envelope Distance** to encapsulate the Stroke.

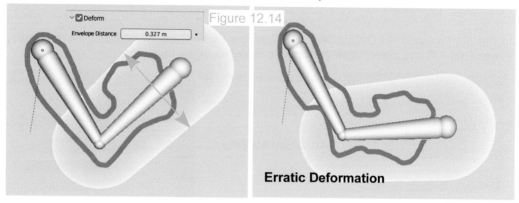

Erratic Deformation

Note: With the Envelope Distance increased part of the Stroke follows the Armature but you will observe that erratic deformation occurs between stroke being influenced by Bone 1 and Bone 2.

One method of improving the deformation is to modify which Vertices are Parented to the Armature Bone by using the **Weight Paint** method. Weight Painting manually Parents Vertices.

Make note that, at this point Bone 2 in the Armature has been selected. Remember a Stroke is made up with a series of Vertices along its centerline. In the initial Parenting process Automatic Weights were applied meaning the Vertices of the Stroke were automatically Parented to the Armature complying with the Field of Influence of the Armature Bones.

To see the assigned Vertices change the Viewport to Object Mode and have the Stroke selected. With the Stroke selected you can change the Viewport to **Weight Paint Mode**. Remember Bone 2 in the Armature was selected while in Pose Mode. In Weight Paint Mode you see the Vertex assignment for Bone 2.

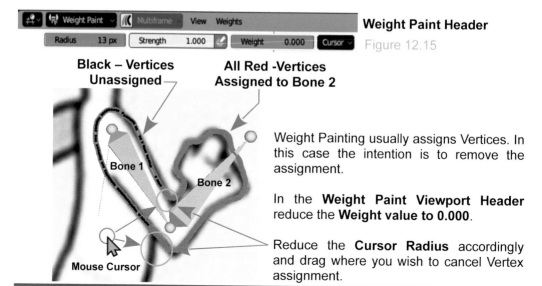

Weight Paint Header

Figure 12.15

Black – Vertices Unassigned

All Red -Vertices Assigned to Bone 2

Weight Painting usually assigns Vertices. In this case the intention is to remove the assignment.

In the **Weight Paint Viewport Header** reduce the **Weight value to 0.000**.

Reduce the **Cursor Radius** accordingly and drag where you wish to cancel Vertex assignment.

Cancelling Vertex assignment reveals the Vertices where you drag the Mouse (Vertices appear black).

Figure 12.16

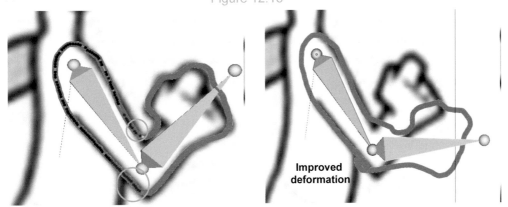

Improved
deformation

Change the Viewport to Object Mode, select the Armature then change to Pose Mode and Rotate Bone 2. The Stroke deformation is improved.

Note: The foregoing is intended to make you aware of the options for Stroke Vertex Assignment to Armatures not to produce a detailed result. There are various methods of employing Armatures for Posing Strokes. Which method you use will depend on your particular application.

12.5 Vertex Groups

Figure 12.17

Bone

Bone.001

Vertex Groups are another way of assigning (parenting) a Stroke's Vertices to an Armature. Vertices are selected in a Stroke and Assigned to a Vertex Group Datablock. The Datablock is Parented to an Armature Bone. When the Bone is Posed the Group of Vertices follow.

Figure 12.18

Properties Editor—➤

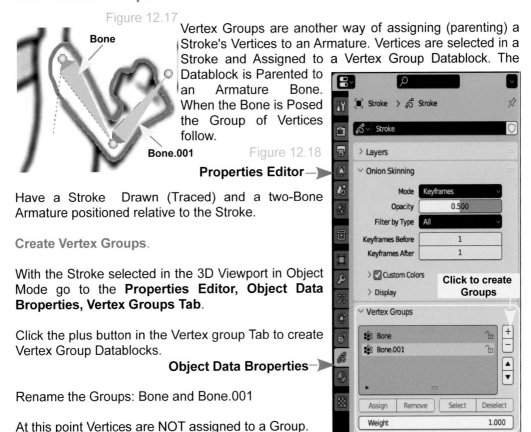

Have a Stroke Drawn (Traced) and a two-Bone Armature positioned relative to the Stroke.

Create Vertex Groups.

With the Stroke selected in the 3D Viewport in Object Mode go to the **Properties Editor, Object Data Broperties, Vertex Groups Tab**.

Click the plus button in the Vertex group Tab to create Vertex Group Datablocks.

Object Data Broperties—➤

Rename the Groups: Bone and Bone.001

At this point Vertices are NOT assigned to a Group.

While in Object Mode select the Stroke then Shift Select the Armature. **Press Ctrl + P** and in the menu that displays select **With Empty Groups**.

The Stroke is Parented to the Armature as seen by the **Armature Modifier** in the Properties Editor Modifier Properties for the Stroke. Figure 12.19

In the Modifier panel change Bind To from Bone Envelopes to **Vertex Groups**.

Since **With Empty Groups** has been employed when Parenting **Vertices have not been assigned.**

In the 3D Viewport, in Object Mode, select the Stroke then Tab into Edit Mode.

Modifier Properties ➙

Have the **Vertex Groups Tab** displayed in the **Properties Editor, Object data Properties** for the Stroke.

Figure 12.20

In the **Vertex Groups** panel click on **Bone.001** to select the Datablock.

In the 3D Viewport, Object Mode, select the Stroke.

Tab into Edit Mode. With **Select Mode, Only Points** selected in the Header -

Select the Stroke again. | **Note:** Buttons are inoperable until Vertices are selected.

Vertices display as black dots indicating that they are NOT selected. Using the **Circle Select Tool** (press the C Key) drag the Mouse over the Stroke selecting Vertices (Vertices turn orange).

In the **Vertex Groups Tab** click **Assign** (Assigns the selected Vertices to Bone.001 (the selected Datablock).

Figure 12.21

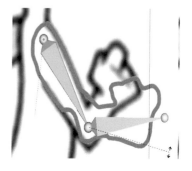

Go into Object Mode. Select the Armature. Go into Pose Mode. Select Bone 2 (Bone.001) and Rotate to see the Vertices (the Stroke) follow.

12.6 Armature Keyframing Exception

Keyframing and **Posing Armatures** for Animation is similar to that described in Chapter 10, Section 10.11, with one exception.

When using Armatures to Pose Strokes, with or without Automatic Keyframing engaged, Keyframes **Do NOT** appear in the **Dope Sheet Timeline Editor** while it is in the **default Grease Pencil Mode.**

Dope Sheet Editor

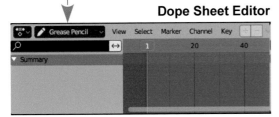

Figure 12.22

To see Keyframes in the **Dope Sheet Editor** change from Grease Pencil Mode to **Dope Sheet Mode.**

Dope Sheet Editor

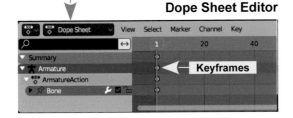

Figure 12.23

The **Timeline Editor** does display **Keyframes.**

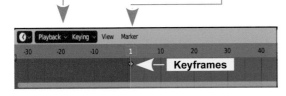

Figure 12.24

13

Creating New Scenes

In Chapter 5, The Canvas Explained, it was demonstrated that a Blender File (.blend) contains data which you save to a Folder on your computer for future use as you work or as the final production. When creating a 2D Animation the Data for the Strokes forming Characters and Scenery are housed in Layers within a Collection. In complex Animations you may have several Collections. All of this data is displayed diagrammatically in the **Outliner Editor** in <u>**View Layer Display Mode**</u>.

Figure 13.1

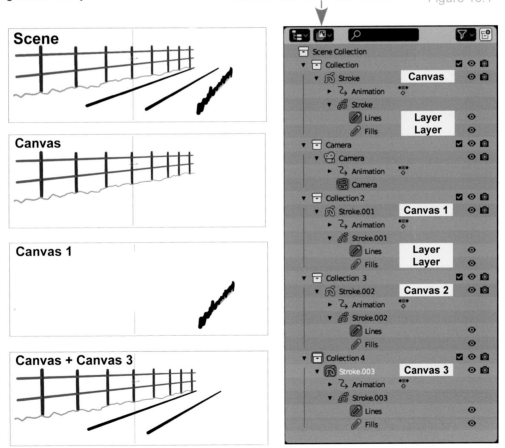

This arrangement of Data into Collections, Canvases and Layers constitutes the Data to produce one Scene in an Animation.

The data for the Scene is saved in the Blender File being worked. When creating an Animation it is common to have multiple Scenes.

Four Scenes in a Animation Figure 13.2

As you watch a Movie you will observe that it changes from one view to another as the story unfolds. You will see close up shots, long shots and shots from varying angles. The different shots produce effects and add to the atmosphere of the story.

The Data displayed in Figure 13.1 (multiple Canvases in multiple Collections) is contained in a single **Scene** in a Blender File and if Animated would Render into a single Video File. It follows that to produce different shots to make up a Movie you would create multiple Blender files. This is not the case, since you can have **Multiple Scenes** in a Blender File.

Outliner Editor Figure 13.3

Figure 13.3 shows the Outliner Editor with the Data for Scene displayed in Figure 13.1 minimized.

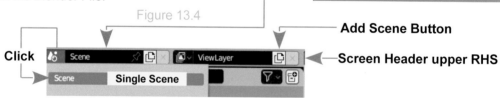

Click the triangles to Expand / Collapse the data display.

In the **Screen Header** you will see the **Single Scene** in the Blender File.

Figure 13.4

Add Scene Button

Click

Screen Header upper RHS

13.1 Adding a Scene

To add a **New Scene** to the Blender File click the **Add Scene Button** and select **New**.

When **New** is selected a New Scene is added to the Blender File; however, the 3D Viewport displays black and the Outliner Editor is empty except for the single entry **Scene Collection**. There is no Canvas or Layers. In the Screen Header you see **Scene.001**.

Figure 13.5

Figure 13.6

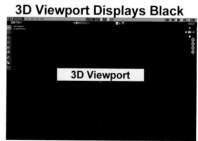

3D Viewport Displays Black

A new Scene has been entered in the Blender File.

The Scene is completely empty of any Data.

Remember: It was suggested that, when you start a new Grease Pencil File, you should leave the default Collection in place.

To create Datablocks for the new Scene go back to Scene and under Scene Collection copy Collection to the clipboard. Change to the new Scene.001, select Scene Collection (RMB Click) and Paste Data Blocks to insert Collection.001 with its Canvas Stroke.001 and Layers, Lines and Fills.

One more step: In the **Properties Editor, World Properties**, click **New** and in the **Surface Tab** change the Color to **White**.

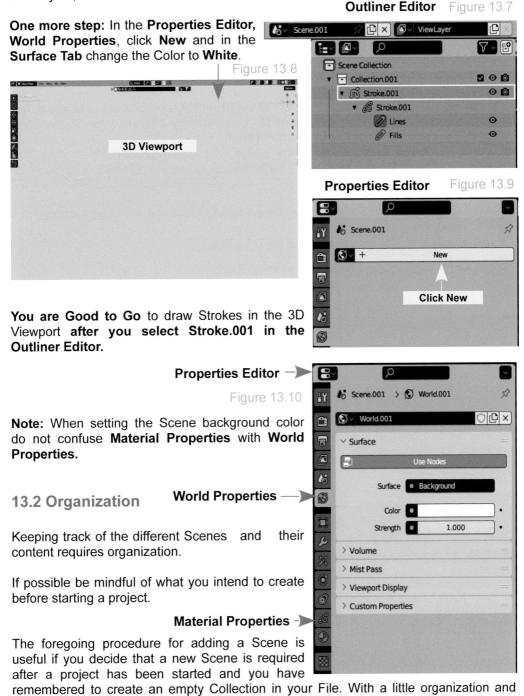

Outliner Editor Figure 13.7

Figure 13.8

3D Viewport

Properties Editor Figure 13.9

Click New

You are Good to Go to draw Strokes in the 3D Viewport **after you select Stroke.001 in the Outliner Editor.**

Properties Editor →

Figure 13.10

Note: When setting the Scene background color do not confuse **Material Properties** with **World Properties.**

13.2 Organization   **World Properties** →

Keeping track of the different Scenes   and   their content requires organization.

If possible be mindful of what you intend to create before starting a project.

Material Properties →

The foregoing procedure for adding a Scene is useful if you decide that a new Scene is required after a project has been started and you have remembered to create an empty Collection in your File. With a little organization and planning the process is simplified.

To demonstrate the logic of the process the simple Animation Sequence of Perpetual Motion created in Chapter 10 Section 10.9 will be employed.

The Perpetual Motion Sequence saw a Ball bouncing around inside a Circle in a 30 Frame Animation (30 Frames at 24 Frames per second (default Frame Rate) = 1.25 seconds of Animation).

13.3 The Storyboard

With any Animation you have to be mindful of the final outcome. A short 1.25 seconds may be what you want. Think of any TV commercial. Some displays on the Screen are even shorter than this. For this demonstration the sequence will be extended.

The plan will be to create three video clips which eventually combine into a single movie file. Let's say have the Ball bounce around for approximately 3.75 seconds (30 frames at 24 Frames per second times three) which will be the first clip (Scene 1). The second clip will see a second ball introduced to the Scene with both bouncing for another 3.75 seconds (Scene 2) followed by more Balls bouncing for yet another 3.75 seconds (Scene 3).

When combined the clips will produce a Video File which will play for 11.25 seconds.

This plan constitutes the **Storyboard** for the production.

As the Video plays additional Bouncing Ball displays are added. Figure 13.11

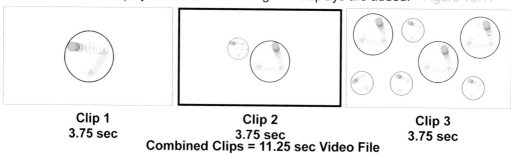

Clip 1	Clip 2	Clip 3
3.75 sec	**3.75 sec**	**3.75 sec**

Combined Clips = 11.25 sec Video File

The Blender File created in Chapter 10 with the Perpetual Motion Animation Sequence has all the Data in one Scene.

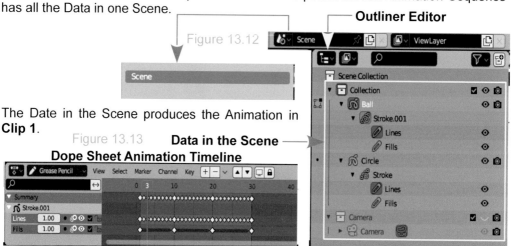

The Date in the Scene produces the Animation in **Clip 1**.

Figure 13.13 **Data in the Scene**

Dope Sheet Animation Timeline

At this point, playing the Animation sees the Ball bounce in the Circle, repeating every 1.25 seconds (30 frames at 24 F/sec). The End Frame in the Timeline = 30 Frames.

To produce the combined Video File playing for 11.25 seconds each Clip has to play for 3.75 seconds, therefore, the sequence in the Timeline has to be extended.

13.4 Extending the Sequence

With the Mouse Cursor in the Timeline Editor, press the B Key (Box Select) and drag a rectangle around the Keyframes (Figure 13.14). Press the D Key (Duplicate) and drag the selection aligning the first Frame of the selection with Frame 31 in the Timeline (Figure 13.15).

Figure 13.14

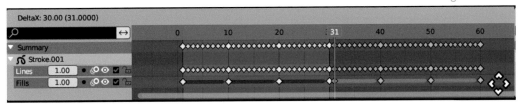

Figure 13.15

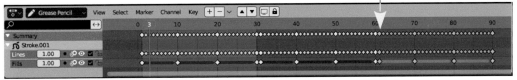

Repeat the duplication aligning the first Frame with Frame 61.——— Figure 13.16

In the **Timeline Editor Header** change the **End Frame to 90** Frames creating a sequence of 90 / 24 = 3.75 seconds.

Figure 13.17

Extending the sequence has increased Clip 1 to 3.75 seconds in the Scene.

To continue, two additional Scenes will be created in the Blender File, initially replicating the original Scene with the extended Animation Sequence.

The Data in the additional Scenes will be modified then the Scenes Rendered (Converted) into Video Files. The Video Files will finally be exported as a Movie File. The following diagram will assist in visualizing the sequence of operations in the process.

13.5 Operation Sequence

Scene 1 (Scene)   Figure 13.18

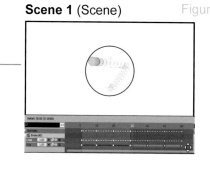

Note: Default Blender Names.

Scene 2 (Scene.001) ◄

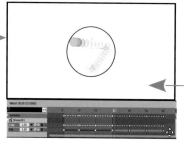

Scene 3 (Scene.002)

At each duplication note the addition to the **Timeline** and the content of the **Outliner Editor.**

In the **Blender Screen Header** click the **New Scene Button** and select **Full Copy**

Selecting **Full Copy** creates Scene 2
Repeat creating Scene 3

Select Scene 2 (Scene.001) in the menu. Box select the Circle and the Ball. Press Shift +D (Duplicate), drag the Mouse to **position and S Key, Scale down**.

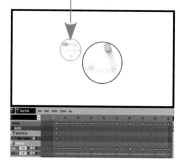

Select Scene 3 (Scene.002) in the menu. Repeat the duplication procedure several times, repositioning duplicates at random.

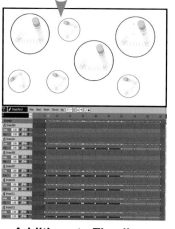

Additions to Timeline

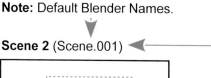

144

With the three Scenes in the Blender File, each Scene would be Rendered, that is, the Animation Sequence would be converted to a Video File format. Following conversion the Video Files would be combined in the Video Editor and exported as a Movie File.

Wrap Up and Render

To wrap it up and complete the process, is to draw Strokes, to Model your Character in a Scene and generate an **Animation Sequence**. Finally you will want to share your work with your friends and showcase it to the world. You will want to **Render** your animation into a **Video File** or convert a **Frame** of the animation into an **Image File**. Video Files may be referred to as **Movie** Files.

Rendering is the process of converting the Blender file information into an **Image file** or a **Video file**. In practice this entails taking the data producing what you see in **Camera View** in the 3D Viewport Editor and converting it into **Image** or **Video file format**. In the Grease Pencil, by default, Camera View is what you see in the 3D Viewport Editor when you first enter the Grease Pencil 2D Animation Workspace. Zoom out slightly to see the limits of Camera View (White Rectangle).

The 3D Viewport Editor   Figure 14.1

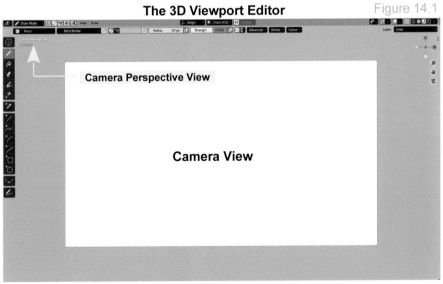

Note: The default **3D Viewport Editor** is in **Camera Perspective View**

After Rendering, the conversion may be viewed as a digital still image or in the case of an Animation Sequence a video file, which will play in a media player. How you view the Render will depend on the Render Output Format chosen. Controls and settings for Rendering are located in the **Properties Editor, Render Properties** and **Output Properties**.

14.1 Render Engines

Render Engines are computer processes that convert the display in Camera View on the Computer Screen into a digital Image or Video File format.

There are three separate rendering systems in Blender. One is the Blender **Eevee** system, the second is the **Cycles** system and the third is the **Workbench** system.

This section explains the basic render procedure using the default **Eevee** system limiting the discussion to producing a still image file or video file.

Figure 14.2

14.2 Eevee in the Properties Editor

Controls for the **Eevee Render Engine** are located in the **Properties Editor, <u>Render Properties</u>** and **<u>Output Properties</u>**.

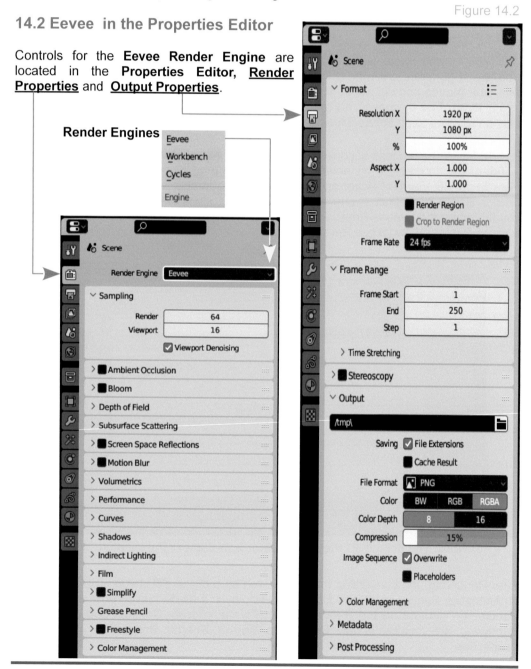

148

14.3 The Render Procedure

At first glance the Controls for Rendering appear daunting, therefore, a demonstration will be limited to a basic procedure.

To demonstrate the procedure for Rendering you must have a Scene created for a still image or an **animation sequence** for a video file.

The **Bouncing Ball Perpetual Motion** sequence created in Chapter 10 – Section 10.9 will be used.

Render Preview: As previously seen, a Render Preview of the Camera View in the 2D Viewport Editor may be viewed by pressing the F12 Key. Pressing F12 displays the **Blender Render** panel showing a Render Result.

Note: What you see in **Blender Render** is a preview only. It is **NOT** a Rendered Image.

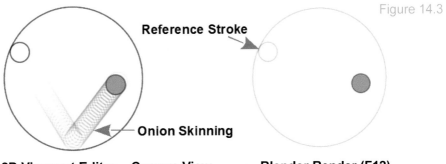

Figure 14.3

2D Viewport Editor – Camera View   **Blender Render (F12)**

In Figure 14.3 **Camera View** and **Blender Render** one Frame of the animation sequence is shown, where the orange ball bounces around inside a circle (Chapter 10 – 10.9). The Camera View shows **Onion Skinning** which does not display in a Rendered View **unless View in Render is checked in the Properties Editor, Object Data Properties, Onion Skinning, Display Tab**. The circle opposite the orange ball is a reference Stroke for the start of the animation.

14.4 Rendering

The first step in Rendering is to set the **Sampling** required (Figure 14.4).

Samples: are the number of paths to trace (computations to perform) for each pixel in the render. As more samples are taken the Render Preview becomes less noisy and more accurate.

Render Properties

Figure 14.4

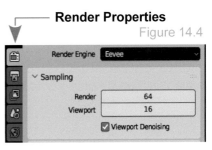

In this demonstration the default values will be used but, the thing to bear in mind is: the more samples, the better the output with regard to clarity and definition of the image but having more samples incurs more computer power and more time. This is not a concern when rendering a single image but with many Frames in an animation the increase in time can be considerable. The second step in rendering is to go to the **Properties Editor, Output Properties.**

In the **Output Properties** you configure the **Resolution** and **Aspect Ratio** for the Image in the **Format Tab** and set the **Output File Format** in the **Output Tab**.

Figure 14.5

The Format Tab

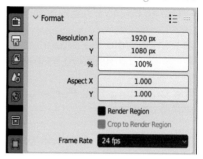

The **Format Tab** (Figure 14.5) is where you tell Blender how big to make your image, the shape of the image, the quality of the image (Resolution) the shape of the pixels (Aspect Ratio) and in the case of an animation where to start and stop rendering and how fast you want it to play back when finished (Frame Rate).

Resolution: **X :** The number of pixels wide in the display. **Y:** The number of pixels high in the display. Higher resolutions mean that there are more pixels per inch (PPI), resulting in more pixel information and creating a high-quality, crisp image.

Aspect Ratio

The Aspect Ratio (Aspect X:Y) of an image is the ratio of its width to its height, usually expressed by two numbers separated by a colon (16:9).

Frame Rate

Note: The **Frame Rate** in the **Properties Editor, Output Properties Format Tab**.

The Frame Rate is the speed of the Animation Playback and the speed of a Video File when an Animation Sequence is Rendered. This requires consideration when exporting a Video for a particular Media such as PAL TV or NTSC TV. Have the default Frame Rate: 24 Frames per Second.

You can leave the default settings for the Resolution and Aspect Ratio for the time being unless you want to get into the serious business of Photographic production. On the other hand **Output File Format** should be given consideration.

The Output Tab Figure 14.6

In the Output Tab you set the file path to a Folder on your PC where you wish Blender to store Render Files. The default Folder is the **tmp** Folder.

In the Windows Operating System this is: **C:\tmp**

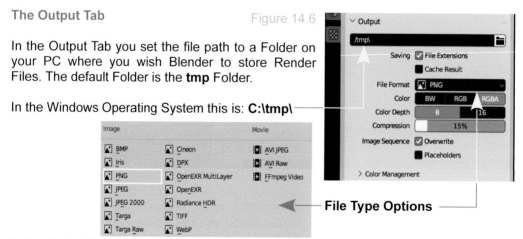

File Type Options

In the **Output Folder** you also select the type of file you wish to save from your Render. The procedure for selection is: You **Render** to the C:\tmp\ Folder then Save an Image or Video File to a location of your choice.

14.5 Rendering an Image

As stated earlier, the first step in Rendering an Image is to set the **Sampling** required (Figure 14.4).

In this demonstration the default values will be used but, bear in mind the previous advice in regard to more samples means more computer power and more time.

The second step in rendering an image is to go to the **Properties Editor, Output Properties Tab** where you configure the **Resolution** and **Aspect Ratio** for the Image in the **Dimensions Tab** and set the **Output File Format**.

With all settings made and the Scene in Camera View, press **F12** on the Keyboard which opens the **Blender Render Image Editor** showing a preview of your image.

In the Editor Header click **Image** and select **Save**. The **Blender File View** panel displays where you navigate to the Folder where you wish to save the image. Click, **Save As Image**, at the bottom of the panel.

14.6 Render a Video File

Figure 14.7

Rendering a Video File is a little different to Rendering an Image. In the Properties Editor, Output Properties, Output Tab you select a Video File Format (AVI JPEG).

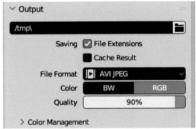

With the first Frame of your Animation Sequence displayed in the 3D Viewport, click on Render in the Header. Select render Animation.

Note: You may also render an Image from this location.

The Blender Render panel displays where you see each Frame of your Animation Sequence display in succession.

Remember the tmp Folder. If you look in the Folder you will find a File with a name something like, 0001-0030.

This PC › Windows: C (C:) › tmp   Figure 14.8

0001-0030

This is in fact an **AVI File** (.avi) the File Format set in the Output Tab. If you play the File in a Video Player, don't blink or you will miss it. The Bouncing Ball Animation is 30 Frames long which, at 24 Frames per Second plays for 1.25 Seconds.

Note: If you have inadvertently selected an Image File Format in the Properties Editor, Output Properties the Render will consist of a series of Image Files saved in the tmp Folder.

14.7 Video Codecs

In the preceding example, changing the default **PNG** file format to **AVI Raw**, you have elected to use the **AVI Raw Video Codec.** This tells the computer how you want your animation data encoded. There are many video Codecs to choose from and simply selecting a Codec type in Blender doesn't necessarily mean that you will get the result that you want. You must have the **Codec** installed on your computer.

A **Codec** is a little routine that compresses the video so that it will fit on a DVD, or be able to be streamed over the internet, or over cable, or just be a reasonable file size.

Simply put, when using a Codec, you encode the Blender animation data to a video file which suits a particular output media such as PAL TV or NTSC TV. When you have used the encoded data to create a video CD or DVD, the CD or DVD is played in a device (CD / DVD Player) which decodes the data for display, in a device such as a Television Screen.

Video Codecs included in Blender

Figure 14.9

One External Codec Source
https://codecguide.com/download_kl.htm   Figure 14.10

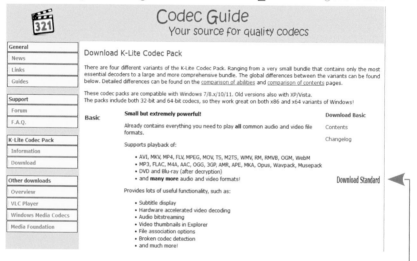

In the **Codec Guide** scroll down to the Standard Pack. Click on **Download Standard.**

In the next page that opens find **Download** and click on **Server 1** to download the installation file.

Figure 14.11

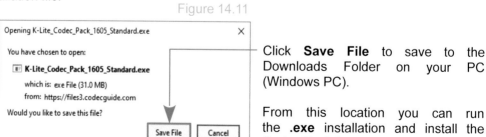

Click **Save File** to save to the Downloads Folder on your PC (Windows PC).

From this location you can run the **.exe** installation and install the Codec Pack to your computer.

Warning: During the Codec Pack installation you are asked to select various options. You will have to research to understand what the options entail before proceeding.

15

Making a Movie

Blender incorporates a complete **Movie Making – Video Editing Workspace**.

Making a Movie is performed in the **Video Sequence Editor** where you compile Video Sequences. The term **Movie** originated from Moving Pictures. Moving Pictures were originally made to entertain and tell stories and this has developed into modern Communication Systems. The basic concept remains, which is, to communicate a story.

Blender provides the tools which allow you to tell your story by using animated pictures (animations). You create Scenes in which actors move depicting events that you wish to communicate to an audience. The animated Scenes are recorded and **Rendered to Movie files**. The individual files are not necessarily produced in a sequence that tells the story, therefore, they need to be arranged in the correct sequence, hence the **Video Sequence Editor**.

15.1 Making a Movie

Making a Movie in Blender will be demonstrated by producing a Video Sequence from a series of short animations which have been rendered to Video Files (Video Clips). The animations may have been created in separate Scenes in a single Blender file or in different Blender files. In either case the animations must be pre-rendered into Video File Format and saved to a folder on your hard drive. The files should preferably be named or numbered in relation to a sequence of events which will tell your story.

15.2 Storyboard

A movie is a visual way of telling a story or communicating a message. To effectively piece together a movie you must have at least an idea of how you want to tell your story. In other words you should have a plan or sketch to use as a reference. The plan is called a **Storyboard**. It is easy to become immersed in the technical detail of the process and lose the plot.

In this demonstration, a submarine on the surface of the ocean, dives underwater and conducts a torpedo attack. The story has been broken down into five parts; Submarine on surface, submarine dives, two underwater views and firing torpedoes. Each part has been animated in a separate Scene in the same Blender file then rendered to an **.AVI video file**.

The video files are all rendered from 250 Frame animations which when combined, equal a movie of 1250 Frames. The movie will be rendered for **PAL TV** which plays at 24 frames per second, therefore, the movie will play for approximately 52 seconds. It is a long way from being a feature film but will give you a basic idea of how a Movie is made.

To demonstrate the process of compiling a Movie work through the procedure as follows. The demonstration will combine the five video files and a sound file.

Sound file? Sound files can be background music, recorded voice, sound effects, and in fact anything to enhance the video. For the purpose of the demonstration a sound file has been compiled in **.wav** format. As with video files there are many types of sound files. You are probably familiar with **MP3 and WAV** etc.

File Path to the Folder containing Video Files

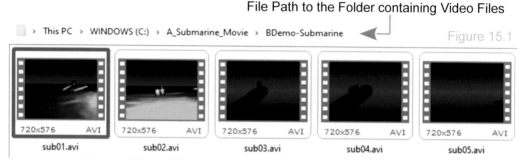

Five .avi Video Files saved in the Folder: **BDemo_Submarine**

15.3 The Sound File

For this demonstration a series of sounds, downloaded from **Free Sounds** at **www.freesound.org**, have been combined (Figure 15.2) using the free program **Audacity.**

Figure 15.2

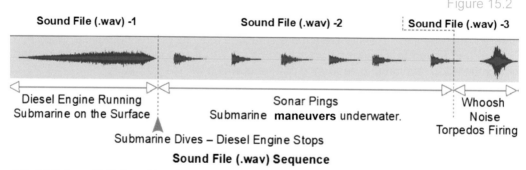

Sound File (.wav) Sequence

15.4 Video Editing Workspace

Video assembly is performed in the **Video Editing Workspace** which is hidden away. In the Screen Header click on **File**, then **New** and select **Video Editing** (Figure 15.3).

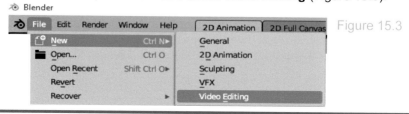

The **Video Editing Workspace** (Figure 15.4). Figure 15.4

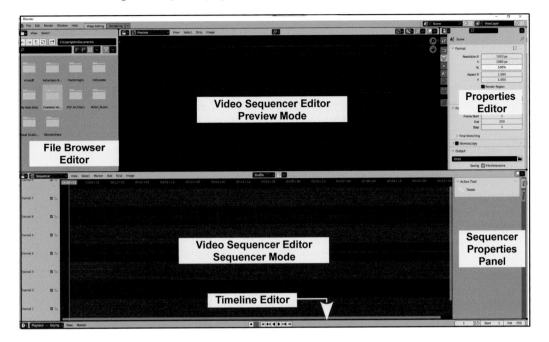

File Browser Editor:	Where you navigate and select files.
VSE Preview Mode:	Where you see the video playback.
Properties Editor:	Controls relevant to the VSE.
VSE Sequencer Mode:	Where you combine Video Files (clips).
Timeline Editor:	Provides control of how the video sequence plays.
Sequencer Properties:	Video Channel Properties (With the Mouse Cursor in the VSE Sequencer Mode press the **N Key** to toggle Hide and Display).

In this basic instruction you will be concerned with the **File Browser Editor** and the **two versions of the Video Sequencer Editor.**

15.5 File Browser Editor

The **File Browser Editor** will be discussed in detail in **Chapter 18** but at this point be aware that the Editor will display files in a variety of ways.

Click to display File Names

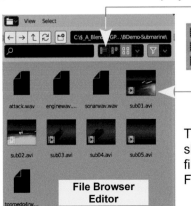

sub01.avi	12 Jul 2009 16:05	296.6 MiB
sub02.avi	12 Jul 2009 16:17	296.6 MiB
sub03.avi	12 Jul 2009 19:36	296.6 MiB

Figure 15.5

First Frame of the Video File (default display).

The default display in the **Video Editing Workspace** shows thumbnail images of the first Frame in each video file (Figure 15.5). You may change the display to show File Names.

15.6 Preparation

File Definition: In this demonstration the five **.avi files** saved to the hard drive will be referred to as **Video Files**. When combined, the final output will be called, the **Movie File**.

Before attacking the **Video Sequencer Editor** some preparation must be performed. The first step in the movie-making process is to set the file path to the location where you want your **Movie File** saved and to define the **Video Output Format**.

Set the File Path for Saving

By default, Blender sets the file path for saving files to the **tmp** (temporary) folder on your hard drive. This can be seen in the **Properties Editor, Output Properties, Output tab** (Figure 15.6).

Change this setting by clicking on the **File Browser** button (Figure 15.6) and navigating to a new folder in the **File Browser Editor**. Select the folder then click on the **Accept button** at the top right-hand side. For convenience and simplicity create a new folder. In this demonstration the folder is named **A_Submarine_Movie** and the file path to the folder is: **C:\ A_Submarine_Movie** (Figure 15.7).

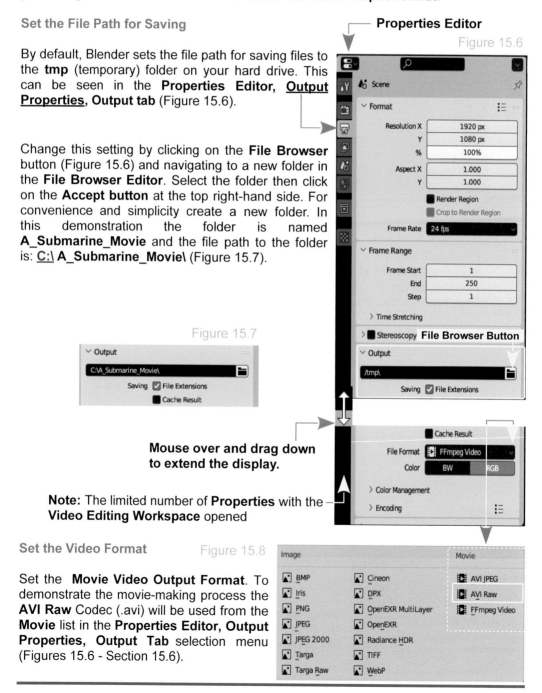

Mouse over and drag down to extend the display.

Note: The limited number of **Properties** with the **Video Editing Workspace** opened

Set the Video Format

Set the **Movie Video Output Format**. To demonstrate the movie-making process the **AVI Raw** Codec (.avi) will be used from the **Movie** list in the **Properties Editor, Output Properties, Output Tab** selection menu (Figures 15.6 - Section 15.6).

Since the **Video Files** (clips) being compiled into a **Movie File** are also **.avi file format** you are, in fact, simply assembling the files into a single file. If you select either the AVI JPEG or FFmpeg video options then the output after assembling would undergo a conversion.

15.7 Video Sequencer Editor

Figure 15.9

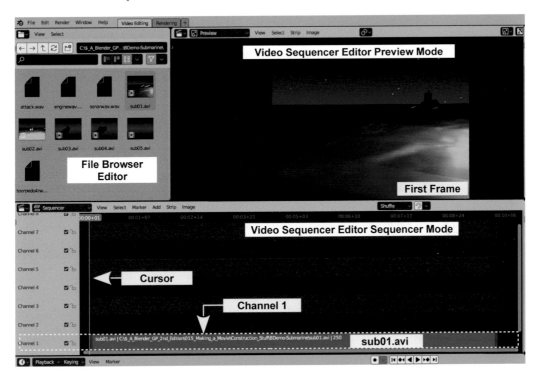

The **Video Sequencer Editor (VSE) Sequencer Mode** is divided into Channels (horizontal strips), numbered at the left-hand side. In Figure 15.9 a Video File named **sub01.avi** has been entered in **Channel 1**. The Video File displays as a blue strip. The vertical blue line in the Editor Panel is the VSE Cursor.

With the Cursor at the Start (left-hand end of the blue strip - Video File) a Preview of the first Frame in the Video File displays in the **VSE Preview Mode** panel above.

Placing Files in the VSE   Figure 15.10

Video Files in the File Browser

Click LMB, Hold and Drag into a VSE Channel.
Hold LMB, drag LR, Up-Down to position.

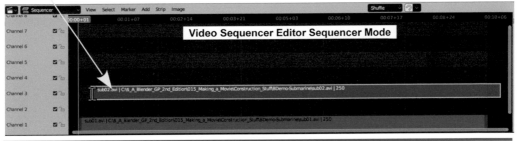

Placing Files in the VSE (Alternative Method)

Various types of files may be entered in the VSE and combined with video files.

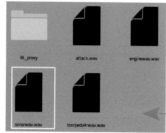

Click on **Add** in the **VSE Header** (Figure 15.11) and select the **File Type** to add. (sonarwav.wav Sound File) in the File Browser Editor. The File will be entered in the VSE in the next available Channel positioned at the VSE Cursor.

File Browser Editor   Figure 15.11

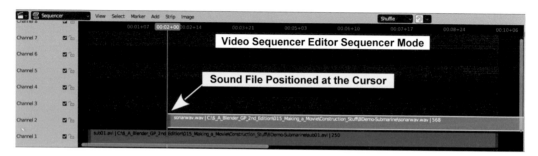

Viewing the Video File

To see Video Files in action click the Play button in the Timeline Editor at the bottom of the Screen. You may also click, hold and drag the VSE Cursor to scrub through the Video Files. Video Files in upper Channels take precedence and play over lower Channels.

Selecting in the VSE

You select a File in a Channel by clicking LMB. Hold and drag R or L to reposition. LMB click on a file, hold and drag up or down to place the file in a different Channel.

When positioning horizontally you will see a **Frame Number** appear at the beginning and end of the Video File giving you the exact location in the Timeline.

Frame Number   **Mouse Cursor**

Figure 15.12

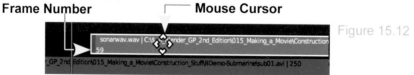

Timeline Graduations / Position   Figure 15.13

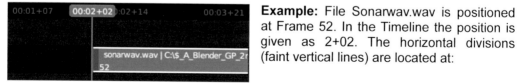

Example: File Sonarwav.wav is positioned at Frame 52. In the Timeline the position is given as 2+02. The horizontal divisions (faint vertical lines) are located at:

0+00 = 50   1.00 = Frame 25   2.00 = Frame 50
(25 Frames per Division)
Frame 52 is, therefore, 2 + 02 = 2 x 25 + 2 = 52

Erasing (Deleting) a File

LMB click on the File in the VSE (border highlights white), press the **X Key** or press Delete or RMB click and select delete.

The Add Button Figure 15.14

The Add button in the VSE Sequencer Mode Panel header contains several options. For example:

Scene: Adds a strip containing information about a Scene.

Mask: If a mask has been created it can be added to the VSE to hide or alter the appearance of parts of the video.

Sound: Sound Files may be inserted in the VSE.

Image/Sequencer: A still image or a series of images may be inserted into the video much like adding individual frames of an animation or a slide show.

Effects Strip: Effects to provide enhancement.

Adding Video Files

When adding Video Files it is helpful to scale and pan the VSE Editor. This allows you to get a bigger picture of your assembly. With the Mouse Cursor in the VSE Editor you can zoom in and out by pressing the Plus and Minus keys on the keyboard or by scrolling MMB.

At the bottom of the VSE Sequencer is a gray bar with faint dots at each end. Click on the bar, hold and drag left or right to pan the display in the VSE. Click hold and drag the dots at either end to scale the VSE view horizontally. A similar vertical pan and scale bar is at the RHS of the VSE.

Movie Files are added to the VSE by clicking, holding and dragging from the File Browser Editor or clicking **Add** in the **VSE Editor header** (Press Add – Movie – navigate in the **File Browser window** – select etc.). The files can be moved to different channels as you wish and positioned horizontally.

Figure 15.5 shows three AVI Files randomly placed in the VSE. Dragging the VSE Cursor over the Files will display Frames from each File in the VSE Preview Mode. In this case, sub03.avi , sub01.avi. sub02.avi. This is a random order not the consecutive order of the Movie. Figure 15.15

159

To have two Movie Files play end-to-end as a continuous sequence, position the start of the second file horizontally at the end of the first file (they do not have to be in the same Channel). With the second file selected, press the **G Key** and drag the Mouse. You will see Frame Numbers display at the beginning and end of each file which makes it easy to align exact Frames. You can purposely overlap files since a file in a higher Channel will take precedence over a file in a lower Channel when playing.

Playing the Video File

No matter where the file is located you can view different Frames in the file by dragging the Cursor along the Timeline. You play the file by pressing the **Start button** in the **Timeline Editor**. Press **Esc** to quit or Pause, Fast Forward etc. by using the play controls.

To mention some more obvious information about playing consider this: the Video Files used in the demonstration are 250 Frames long. With the first located with the **Start Frame** at 0+01 it will play in its entirety then repeat until you press **Esc**. This only occurs since, in the **Timeline Editor**, **Start: 1** and **End: 250** are set. If **End: 100** was set the file would only play for 100 Frames then repeat, or if the start Frame of the file was positioned on the VSE Timeline other than at Frame 1 then only part of the file will play. (see Figure 15.16).

File in the <u>Upper Channel</u> Plays over the Lower Channel

Figure 15.16

**Selected File Information
Press N Key
Toggle Hide/Display**

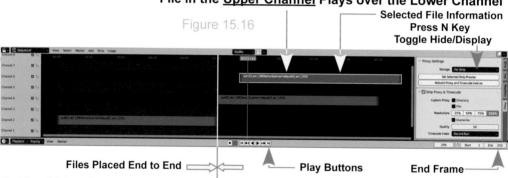

Files Placed End to End ⟶⟵   Play Buttons   End Frame

Cutting Video Strips

A Video File in the VSE is also referred to as a **Video Strip**. Another feature of the VSE is the ability to select only part of a video strip for playback. You can cut the strip into segments. There are two ways to do this: a **Soft Cut** and a **Hard Cut**. In either case, position the Cursor at the Frame where you wish to make the cut. For a **Soft Cut** press the **K Key**.

For a **Hard Cut** press **Shift + K key**. In either case you finish up with two separate segments of strip which you can reposition or move to a different Channel in the VSE. The difference is, with a **Soft Cut** both segments of the strip retain the data for the other part. With a **Hard Cut** the data is not retained (Figure 15.17).

Figure 15.17

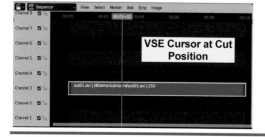

VSE Cursor at Cut Position

Select File – Press Shift + K key to Cut

Adding Sound Files

Sound files such as MP3 and WAVE are entered by dragging from the File Browser or selecting **Sound** in the **Add button menu** instead of **Movie** and then manipulating the same as a Video File.

With all your strips aligned and edited you can press the **Play button** in the **Timeline Editor** to preview the final movie. Don't forget to have your sound system turned on.

15.8 Rendering the Movie File

When all the specifications have been set for your Movie Output File it is time to render the final movie.

Figure 15.18

In the **Screen Header** click the **Render button** and select **Render Animation**. Be prepared to wait a considerable time. Even a short movie will take a while depending on the speed of your computer. Long movie sequences are often uploaded to websites called **Render Farms** which will perform the render process for you (at a cost). Once the render is complete you find the file in the output folder.

15.9 Additional Features

Additional features for enhancing and modifying video strips are found in the Video Sequencer Header Add button menu. Generally adding a feature from the Header inserts a special Feature Strip in the VSE.

Example: Adding a Color Strip   Figure 15.19

In the **VSE Header**, click **Add**, select **Color**. A **Color Strip** is inserted in the Sequencer.

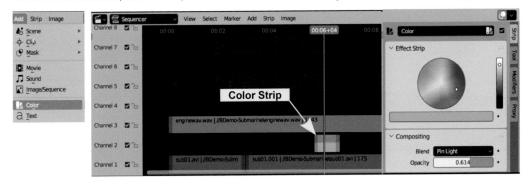

Color Strip

Note: Make sure the Strip is in the Channel above the Video File you wish to enhance. Click LMB on the Strip, hold and drag LR to extend the Strip.

With the Color Strip selected in the VSE controls display in the **Strip Properties** panel at the RHS, select a **Color**. Select a **Compositing Blend Type** and adjust the **Opacity**.

Before   Figure 15.20   **After**

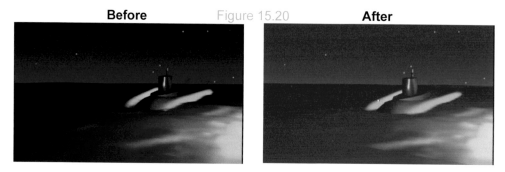

Example: Adding a Color Modifier

Select a Strip in the VSE. In the Strip Properties, Modifiers Tab click Add Strip Modifier. In this case select Color. Alter the values in the color pickers to adjust the preview display. Color is applied permanently for the whole Strip.

Video Sequencer   Figure 15.21   **Strip Properties**

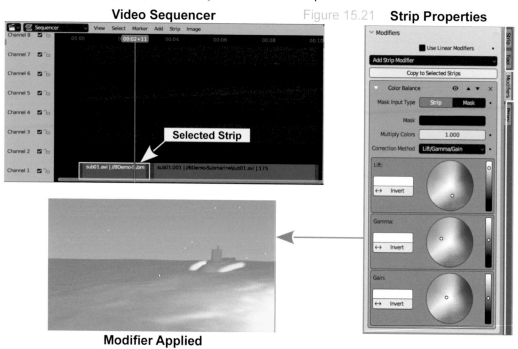

Modifier Applied

Example: Inserting Text Captions   Figure 15.22

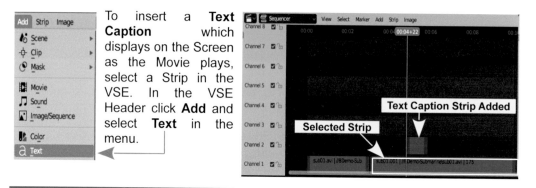

To insert a **Text Caption** which displays on the Screen as the Movie plays, select a Strip in the VSE. In the VSE Header click **Add** and select **Text** in the menu.

Selecting **Text** in the menu inserts a **Text Caption Strip** in a VSE Channel. To have Text display in the Preview make sure the Text Caption Strip is in a VSE Channel **above** the selected Movie Strip. Click, Hold and Drag the end of the Caption Strip to set the length of the display in the Preview

Display Length ←——————→ **Click, Hold, Drag**

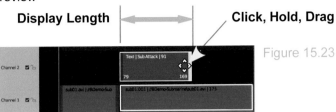

Figure 15.23

With a **Text Strip** inserted in the **VSE** controls display in the **Properties Panel, Strip Tab.**

To see the Text Caption in the Preview Panel position the **VSE Cursor over the Strip.**

Figure 15.24

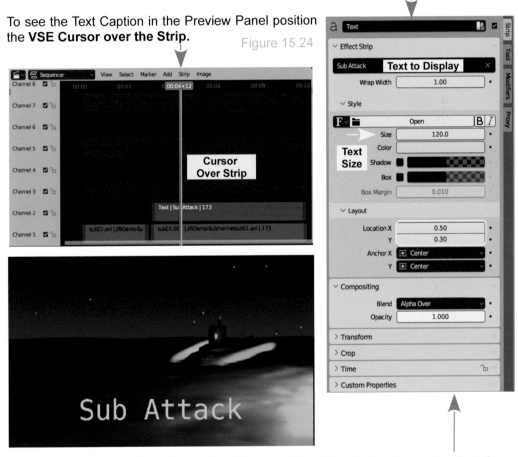

Adjust the Caption Size, Color, Font Type and Position in the Properties Panel

16

Using a Drawing Tablet

In the preceding chapters, how to draw has been demonstrated using a Mouse. A **Drawing Tablet** allows you to draw Strokes using a **Stylus**. This provides the freedom to draw as you would with a pencil on a paper pad. A **Drawing Tablet** is the superior tool for an artist but you should be aware that there is a learning curve to mastering the use of a Stylus. The technical set-up of a Tablet and Stylus is not difficult but training your hand-eye coordination will take practice.

Figure 16.1

Before you can use a Drawing Tablet you have to install the **Driver Software** for your particular device. Make sure you have the latest Driver and follow the instructions provided by the supplier.

With the software installed and the Tablet connected to your computer, Blender will automatically recognize the device. There are no settings in Blender which apply to any specific brand of Tablet. The only settings you may wish to activate are settings for emulating a Three-Button Mouse, specifically allowing you to use keyboard keys in conjunction with a drawing **Stylus** (the Pen that comes with the tablet).

16.1 Emulating a Three-Button Mouse

Placing and moving the tip of the Stylus (Pen) on the surface of the Drawing Tablet replicates clicking, holding and dragging the Mouse to Draw a Stroke on the computer monitor Screen. This does not cancel the use of the Mouse. You may use either device to draw and you may find it easier to select control functions on the Screen using the Mouse click. Both the Stylus and Mouse control the movement of the Cursor on the Screen. Which device you use will develop with practice.

Some Mouse controls require you to press the Middle Mouse Button (MMB). A Stylus may have buttons which can be set to replicate the MMB but if not, checking Emulate 3 Button Mouse in the **Preferences Editor** allows you to control functions from the Stylus in conjunction with Keyboard commands.

16.2 Blender Preferences Editor

To set the Stylus to work with the Keyboard click on **Edit** in the Blender Screen Header and select **Preferences** ,in the menu that displays, to open the **Blender Preferences Editor**.

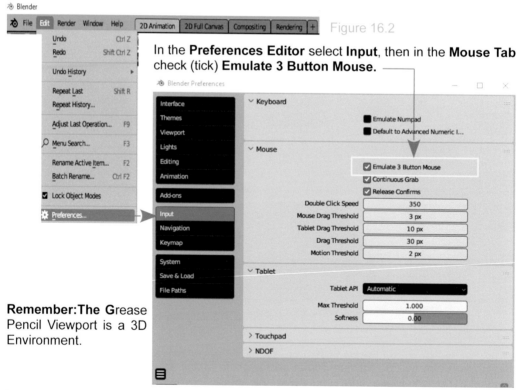

Figure 16.2

In the **Preferences Editor** select **Input**, then in the **Mouse Tab** check (tick) **Emulate 3 Button Mouse.**

Remember:The Grease Pencil Viewport is a 3D Environment.

With a Stroke drawn in the 3D Viewport Editor (Figure 16.3) clicking, holding the MMB and **dragging the Mouse rotates the 2D Viewport.**

Figure 16.3

Stroke Drawn

When using a Stylus on a Drawing Tablet, with **Emulate 3 Button Mouse** activated, holding the **Alt Key** depressed on the Keyboard and moving the Stylus produces the same result.

Also when using a Stylus, holding the **Alt Key** plus the **Ctrl Key** and moving the Stylus up or down Zooms the Viewport in / out. Holding the **Alt Key** plus **Shift** and moving the Stylus pans the Viewport.

16.3 3D Viewport Editor Controls

The following shows a Stroke Line drawn using a Tablet and Stylus. Make note of the **settings in the 3D Viewport Editor Header**.

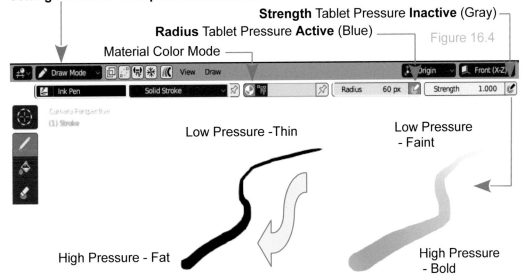

Stroke Line drawn by **increasing pressure** on the Stylus from start to finish.

A similar Stroke Line drawn with the **Strength Tablet Pressure** activated.

In the 3D Viewport Editor Header, by default, **Pressure Sensitivity** is activated for the Radius value such that, as pressure is increased and the Stroke is drawn, the Radius (width) of the Stroke Line increases.

16.4 Tablet Properties

With the software for a Drawing Tablet installed you will have **Tablet Properties** available where you can modify settings to your personal requirements. As an example the properties for a **Wacom Intuos 3D Tablet** will be demonstrated when installed on a **Windows 10 Computer**.

The Properties for the Tablet are accessed by clicking the Windows Start button and opening **All Apps.** Scroll down to **Wacom Tablet**, click LMB and select **Wacom Tablet Properties**.

Alternatively you will find the Properties in **Windows File Explorer**.

Tip: To find the Tablet Properties you must have the Tablet connected and turned on.

16.5 Wacom Tablet Properties

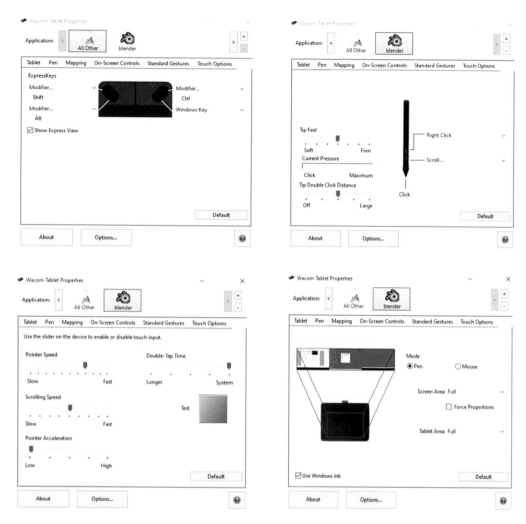

To make settings in the Tablet Properties applicable to Blender only, enter Blender in the Add Application for Custom Settings.

Figure 16.6

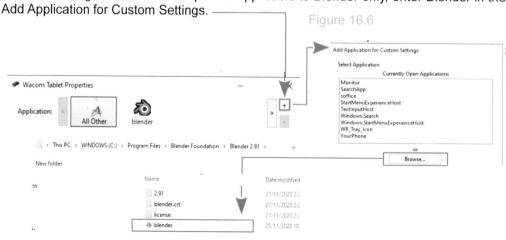

16.6 Drawing Examples using a Tablet

Figure 16.7

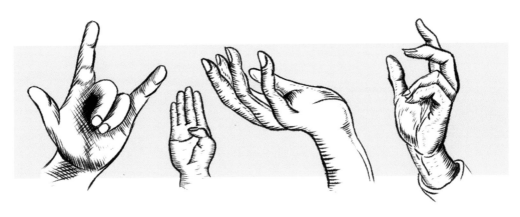

17

Download & Installation

17.1 Blender and the Book

When using instructions provided in this book it is recommended that you use **Blender Version 3.6 LTS 0r later**. Blender is continually being updated with new improvements and additions and consequently new versions of the program are released at intervals. At the time of writing Blender Version 3.6 LTS (Long Term Support) is the current release of Blender with Version 4.0.0 imminent.

Download Blender from: **www.blender.org/download/**   Figure 17.1

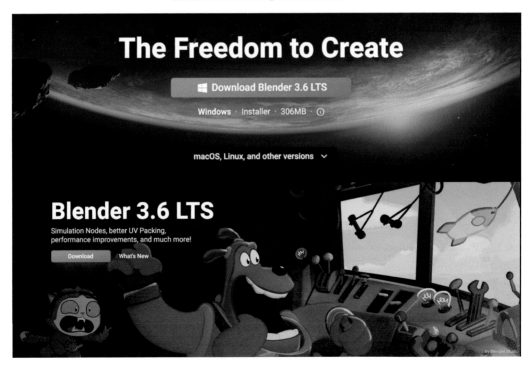

17.2 Download Blender

Clicking the download link downloads the MSI installer for Windows. **Alternatively** select the current **Blender version** which is applicable to your operating system. Blender is available for **Windows, MacOS, Linux and Steam.**

Figure 17.2

Downloading from the main download link presents the option to download the **.msi** installation file.

blender-3.6.0-windows-x64.msi
Completed — 306 MB

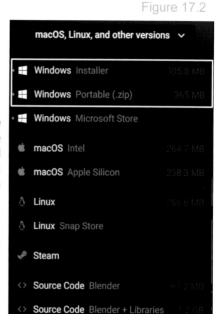

Selecting the **Windows Installer** from the download options menu also presents the same **msi** installer option. Clicking **Save File** will download the installer to your hard drive which on a Windows system is usually to the **Downloads Folder**.

Also in the menu, you have the option to download **Windows Portable (.zip)** which is a compressed ZIP file.

blender-3.6.0-windows-x64.zip

17.3 Installation on a Windows Operating System

Installing with the Installer(.msi) Option

Double click on the file name in the Downloads folder, follow the prompts in the **Setup Wizard** and Blender will be automatically installed to the **Program Files** folder on your computer and a <u>shortcut icon will be placed on your **Desktop**</u>.

Figure 17.3

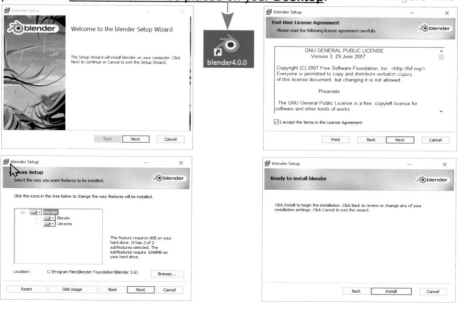

17.4 Installing the ZIP Option

With a **ZIP file** you have to unzip the file. First **create a New Folder on your computer's hard drive** then use a program such as 7-Zip, WinRAR or WinZip to unzip (decompress) the zip file into the new folder.

If you have a program, such as WinRAR, installed on your computer, double clicking the ZIP file in the Downloads Folder automatically opens the ZIP in WinRAR where you extract the program to a folder on your PC.

Click Extract To and select a Folder

Figure 17.4

WinRAR

When the file is unzipped into the new folder and the folder opened, you will see **blender.exe** as one of the entries. You double click on this to run Blender or you create a shortcut which places a shortcut icon on your desktop.

When using either installation option you double click the **blender.exe** file to run the program. Shortcuts on the Desktop are shortcuts to the blender.exe file.

Note: By having one version of Blender installed via the Installer (.msi) option and another version using the ZIP method you can have more than one Blender version installed on your computer at the same time. This is useful for version comparison or for development purposes.

17.5 Installing Blender on a Linux Operating System

Ubuntu

http://www.wikihow.com/Install-Blender-3D-on-Ubuntu

Debian 8 (Jessie)

https://www.howtoinstall.co/en/debian/jessie/blender

Installing Blender on MacOS

https://wiki.blender.org/wiki/Building_Blender/Mac

You may also install earlier versions of the Blender program which will allow you to follow instructions available on the internet written in that version of Blender.

17.6 Installing Earlier Blender Versions (Windows operating system)

When attempting Blender for the first time by following a tutorial, whether it is a book, a written tutorial or a video tutorial, always look at the Blender version for which it is written and work through examples using that version. It is tempting to grab the latest Blender version but consider the information given in the tutorial, as a training exercise then step up to the latest developments in the current release.

For earlier versions of Blender see:
https://www.blender.org/download/previous-versions/   Figure 17.5

Figure 17.6

The Earlier Release Index contains both the MSI Installer and the ZIP options. Installation previously described.

17.7 Running (Opening) Blender

To run Blender, double click the shortcut icon on your desktop or navigate to the folder on your hard drive (see over) to find the **blender.exe** file and double click the file.

File Explorer   Figure 17.7

> This PC > Windows: C (C:) > Program Files > Blender Foundation > Blender 3.5

	3.5	18/06/2023 8:22 AM
	blender.crt	18/06/2023 8:23 AM
	blender.shared	18/06/2023 8:23 AM
	license	18/06/2023 8:23 AM
	blender **Blender.exe**	25/04/2023 2:11 AM
	blender.pdb	25/04/2023 1:56 AM
	blender_debug_gpu	15/02/2023 5:45 PM

Desktop Shortcut Icon

18

Navigate and Save

18.1 Saving Work

When you work in Blender you edit (modify) the default file which opens when you start Blender or a file that has been previously saved. Blender file names end with a **.blend** suffix and are peculiar to the Blender program. Saving work means you save the modifications or editing, that has been performed in a Blender file. You save the file, in a folder of your choice on your computer's hard drive. You should understand how and where to create a folder and how to retrieve a file when it has been saved. In other words you need to know how to navigate your file system. In Blender files are saved on your computer using the **File Browser Editor**.

In Blender you create files and store them away for future use. You can reuse the files and build on to them and then save the new material. Saved files are your library of information from which you extract elements and insert into future work. The saying is, **"There is no point reinventing the wheel"**. If you have created something that works use it again. But where did you put the wheel? That's where navigation comes in. You need to find the place where you safely stored that wheel or, in the case of Blender, where you saved a file containing the wheel.

Navigation in Blender is performed in the **File Browser Editor** or in its subsidiary **Blender File View.**

Before looking at either File Browser or File View you should understand the definitions of Files and Folders.

18.2 Files and Folders

Definition (from the internet)

A file is a common storage unit in a computer, and all programs and data are "written" into a file and "read" from a file. A folder holds one or more files, and a folder can be empty until it is filled. A folder can contain other folders (sub-folders). Folders provide a method for organizing files much like a manila file folder contains paper documents in a file cabinet. In fact, files that contain text are often called documents.

Folders are also called "directories," and they are created on the hard drive (HD) or solid state drive (SSD) when the operating system and applications are installed.

Files are always stored in folders. In fact, even the computer desktop is a folder; a special kind of folder that displays its contents across the entire screen.

File Extensions

A file extension or suffix, is the bit at the end of a file name preceded by a dot or period. For example, My_Photo**.JPEG**, would be a JPEG image (photograph). The **.JPEG** extension tells the computer which application (App) or program to use when opening the file. With a **.JPEG** extension the computer would look for an image editor or viewer to open the file. With a **.TXT** extension, signifying a text file, the computer would use a text editor.

When writing file extensions to a file name they are usually written in lower case letters such as **.jpeg** or **.txt**.

Blender files have a **.blend** extension which tells the computer to open the file in the Blender program.

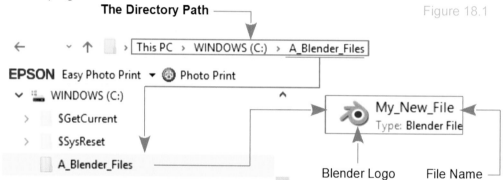

Figure 18.1

Windows 10 File Explorer

Figure 18.1 shows a Blender file saved in the **C: Directory** (Hard Drive) in a Folder named **A_Blender_Files**. The Blender file is named **My_New_File**. Blender file names usually display with the Blender logo preceding the file name but the **.blend** file extension does not always display.

18.3 Saving a Blender File

On a computer, when you save a Blender file (.blend) you are saving the data which is producing the display on the computer screen. This set of data includes not only what you see but also all the settings which control all the effects that will be displayed in the various Editors. The Blender File may be considered as a complete package. Saving a file for the default arrangement saves everything.

Figure 18.2 shows the data listed in the **Outliner Editor** which would be saved for the default **Grease Pencil Blender Scene**. **Note**: The Outliner Editor is in **View Layer Mode**.

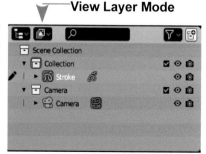

View Layer Mode

Figure 18.2

Note: The default Scene has not been Edited. Strokes have not been Drawn or Objects Added.

You may consider it a Blank Canvas.

Even as a Blank Canvas you Save the File which can then be retrieved for future work.

In the **Screen Header** click on **File** and select **Save As**.

Figure 18.3

The **Blender File View** panel displays. In the LH Column of File View click on **Windows C (C:)** to display Folders in the C: Drive.

With the Mouse Cursor in the RH Column, scroll down and find the Folder where you wish to save your File (**A_Blender_Files**).

Blender File View

Figure 18.4

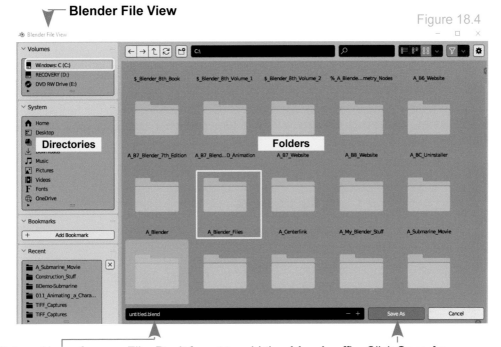

Enter a Name for your File. Don't forget to add the **.blend** suffix. Click **Save As**.

In **Blender File View** you select **Directories** in the LH Column and select **Folders** in the RH Column. Finding Files in Directories is Navigating the File System.

18.4 Navigating the File System

To Navigate the File System it helps if you understand the meaning of the File System. Basically the File System is the arrangement of Partitions, Directories, Folders and Files saved on the Computer's Drive. Drives come in a variety of flavors.

Figure 18.5

To start with, your computer has a Disk Drive. Probably a Hard Disk or Solid-State (SSD). The Drive is **Partitioned**, meaning it is digitally divided into parts for storing different types of Data. The **Partitions** may be viewed in your **Disk Management**.

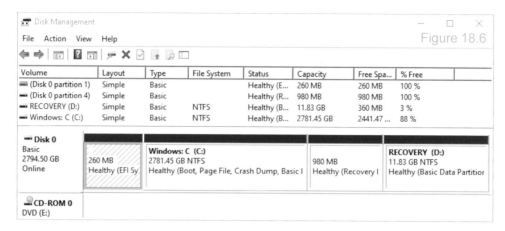

Figure 18.6

You will be mainly concerned with Windows: C (C:) Drive which itself is further divided into Directories containing Folders which in turn contain Files. This may be viewed diagrammatically:

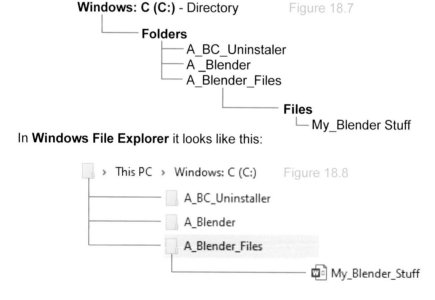

Figure 18.7

In **Windows File Explorer** it looks like this:

Figure 18.8

In the **Blender File View Header** (Figure 18.9) there are controls for **Navigating the File System.**

Figure 18.9

Previous Folder

Next Folder

Parent Directory

Refresh the File List

Display Mode Options

18.5 The File Browser Editor

To understand the File System, compare the **Blender File Browser Editor** to **Windows File Explorer**. The Blender File View is a mini version of the Blender File Browser.

Blender File Browser Editor　　Figure 18.10

LMB click on a Directory to display Folders in the Directory

Windows File Explorer　　Figure 18.11

Note: The Blender File Browser Editor Header has the same controls as the Blender File View panel.

Note: You **CAN NOT** open Files in the File Browse Editor. To open Files click **File** in the Header then **Open** which displays **Blender File View**. Navigate to the File then double click the File.

Important: Be aware that **Blender File View** displays Directories and Folders but only displays Files which can be opened in Blender that is Files with the **.blend** suffix (Blender Files).

19

Using Add-ons

Add-ons are additional Blender functions which you activate when required. Blender includes a variety of Add-ons hidden away in the **User Preferences Editor** and there are literally hundreds available for download from the internet. Add-ons are pieces of computer code written in the **Python** programming language (Python Scripts).

The Blender website contains a link to a scripts repository where a vast number of Add-ons can be found, however, since the Grease Pencil is a relatively new development, Add-ons specific to the Grease Pencil are limited.

All Add-ons, when downloaded, have to be installed in the **User Preferences Editor.**

The Grease Pencil has one Add-on pre-installed in the program but to use this Add-on, it has to be activated. To activate the Add-on and see Blender's list of Add-ons click **Edit** in the Screen Header and select **Preferences** in the menu.

Figure 19.1

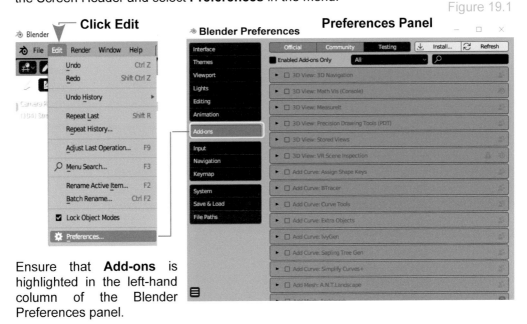

Ensure that **Add-ons** is highlighted in the left-hand column of the Blender Preferences panel.

Note: The **Blender Preferences Panel** accessed via the Edit button in the Screen Header is an abbreviated version of the **Preferences Editor** accessed from the **Editor Version button** in the 3D Viewport Header.

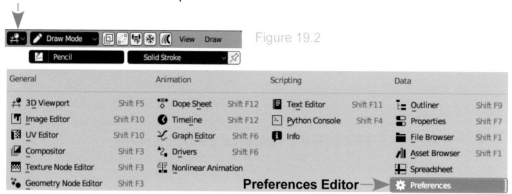

Figure 19.2

Selecting the **Preferences Editor** replaces the 3D Viewport Editor in the Screen display. Selecting the **Preferences Panel** via the Edit button opens the Blender Preferences Panel in the Editor being displayed.

19.1 The Included Grease Pencil Add-on

Figure 19.3

To activate the pre-installed Add-on, type **Grease Pencil** in the **Search Bar.**

Note: Be aware that all Add-ons are not equal. They are installed to the User Preferences and all activated by checking (ticking) the activation button. The controls for using an Add-on vary depending on how they have been written.

In the case of the **Object: Grease Pencil Tools** Add-on the controls are located, as stated in the Location in the Information Panel: **Sidebar > Grease Pencil > Grease Pencil Tools**.

Figure 19.4

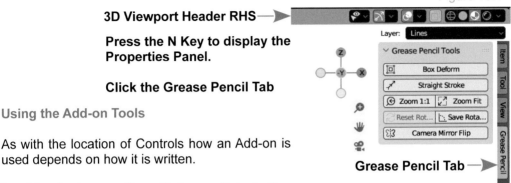

3D Viewport Header RHS───▶

Press the N Key to display the Properties Panel.

Click the Grease Pencil Tab

Grease Pencil Tab───▶

Using the Add-on Tools

As with the location of Controls how an Add-on is used depends on how it is written.

In this instance: Box Deform. Select **Box Deform** in the **Grease Pencil Tools.**

With a Stroke drawn in Draw Mode and then selected in Edit Mode the **Viewport changes** and displays a rectangle on the Stroke.

Figure 19.5

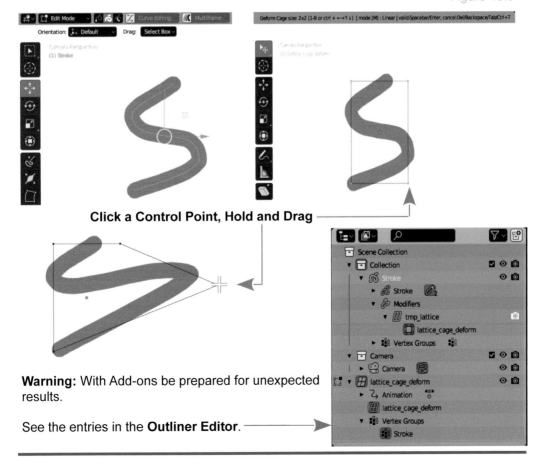

Click a Control Point, Hold and Drag ────────

Warning: With Add-ons be prepared for unexpected results.

See the entries in the **Outliner Editor**. ────▶

19.2 Downloading Add-ons

You may download Add-ons from the internet but remember, they have to be installed.

One source of Add-ons for the Grease Pencil is:

https://github.com/Vencient/PLANEX_Blender

Figure 19.6

To the right of the page click on the green download **Code** button.

In the panel that displays click on **Download ZIP**.

PLANEX_Blender-master   Figure 19.7

The compressed ZIP File is saved in the Downloads Folder.

Create a **new Folder** on your computer. Name the **Folder Planex_Blender** then use an application like WinZIP, WinRAR or 7Zip to unzip (decompress) the File to your Folder. After unzipping you will have a Folder named **PLANEX_Blender-master** containing four Files.

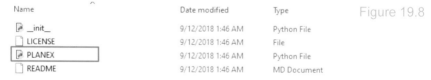

Figure 19.8

The File named **PLANEX** is a Python File (PY File) which you install into Blender.

19.3 Installing the Python File

Open the **Preferences Editor** with **Add-ons** selected in the left-hand panel. In the **Preferences Editor Header** click on **Install**.

Figure 19.9

Clicking **Install** opens the **Blender File View Editor** where you navigate the Folder containing the Python File.

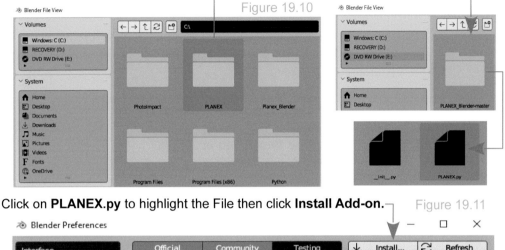

Figure 19.10

Click on **PLANEX.py** to highlight the File then click **Install Add-on.**

Figure 19.11

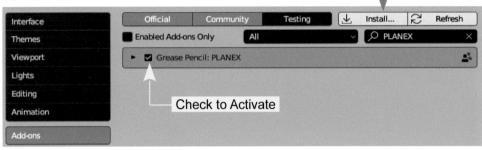

Check to Activate

19.4 Add-on Another Way

Add-ons can be downloaded directly in the Grease Pencil. For example you may add extra Brushes.

In the **Preferences Editor**, **Add-ons**, type **grease** into the search bar and the Add-on named **Object: Grease Pencil Tools** will display. If you have previously installed Grease Pencil: PLANEX it will also display.

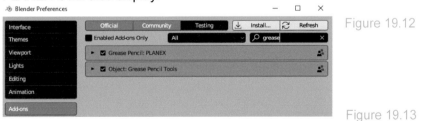

Figure 19.12

Figure 19.13

In the 3D Viewport Editor, **with Object: Grease Pencil Tools active** (checked) **Note: Stroke** in the **Outliner Editor.** This has previously been described as the **Canvas** in which Strokes are Drawn and contains the two Layers named Lines and Fills. Stroke is a **Datablock** containing the information for the Canvas and as such is a **Grease Pencil Object**.

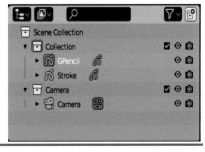

To use the **Object: Grease Pencil Tools Add-on** you must have a Grease Pencil Object in the Blender File. If there is no Grease Pencil Object in the File go to Object Mode and in the 2D Viewport Editor click on **Add – Grease Pencil – Blank**. Doing so, enters a Grease Pencil Object in the Outliner Editor named **GPencil**.

Change the 2D Viewport Editor to Draw Mode. Have **Stroke** or **GPencil** selected in the Outliner Editor.

Figure 19.14

With the **Add-on**, **Object: Grease Pencil Tools** active, press the **N Key** (with the Mouse Cursor in the 2D Viewport Editor) to display the **Object Properties Panel**. **Note: The Grease Pencil Tab** at the RH Side of the Panel. Click the Tab to display options.

With the Add-on **Object: Grease Pencil Tools** active go to the **Properties Editor, Active Tool and Workspace Properties**. In the **Brushes Tab** click **Brush Specials** and in the selection menu click **Download and Import Texture Brush Pack**.

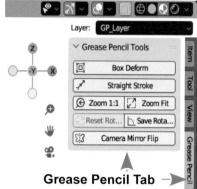

Grease Pencil Tab →

Figure 19.15

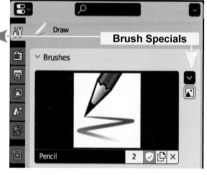

A notification displays at the bottom of the Screen when the download and installation is completed.

16 brushes installed

Brush Specials

Selecting the Brush options in the 3D Viewport Header or in the Properties Editor Brushes tab displays the **Brush Palette** containing the default Brush Types plus the new selection.

Default Brush Selection

Figure 19.16

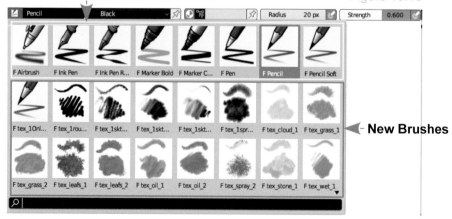

◄ **New Brushes**

Remember: To have the Brush Selection available for future work, **Save a Blender File**.

20

Internet Resources

A Sample of Grease Pencil Resources

https://studio.blender.org/training/grease-pencil-fundamentals/pages/resources/

https://studio.blender.org/training/grease-pencil-fundamentals/

https://www.blendernation.com/2018/11/23/free-downloads-grease-pencil-projects/

https://all3dp.com/2/blender-2d-animation-grease-pencil-simply-explained/

https://blenderartists.org/t/the-big-blender-grease-pencil-thread/1381029

21

Index

A

B

C

Camera 12,57,59
Camera Perspective View 147
Camera View 59,58,63,64,67,147
Cancel the Parenting 133
Canvas 11,12,31,33,57-59,62,64,76
Canvas and Layers 33,59,139
Canvas Center 37
Canvas Explained 57,139
Canvas Grid 74,75,76
Canvas Tab 75
Canvas Volume 63
Caption Size 163
Center of Canvas 33,34,38
Center of Geometry 5,101
Channel 71,157,158,161
Character 6,18,118
Character Animation 119
Chevron 15
Circle of Influence 21,36,101
Circle Select Tool 136
Circle Stroke 61,107
Circle Tool 22,61,107
Clips 142
Closed Stroke 24
Codec 151,152
Codec Guide 152
Codec Pack 152
Codec Source 152
Collection 66,67,72,73,88,139,141
Color Attribute Scheme 51
Color Schemes 25
Color and Palette Tabs 15
Color Attribute 44,48,49,52,70,98,102
Color Attribute Color Scheme 48
Color Attribute Mode 15
Color Attribute Palette 50
Color Fill 43
Color Palette 15,44,48-50
Color Picker Circle 48,50,103
Color Scheme 44,52
Color Selection 26
Color Strip 161
Color Swatch 44
Color Swatches 50
Color Tab 43
Color Workspace 50,51
Coloring and Customizing 43
Coloring and Customizing Strokes 41
Coloring Strokes 25,98
Combining Converting Strokes 102,103

Complex Animations 107
Computer Graphics 8
Conflicting Terminologies 60
Conjoined 130
Control Handle 7,22,27
Control Points 34,35,37
Controlling and Placing Strokes 98
Controls 12-15,75
Controls for Rendering 149
Controls in the 3D Viewport 15
Convert to Mesh 101
Convert to Path 99,103
Converted to a Video File 145
Converting 99
Corrections 6
Create a New Blender File 69
Create a new Brush 53
Create a New Canvas 66
Create Vertex Groups 135
Cube Object 79
Cubic Volume 62
Cursor 78
Cursor and Origin 78
Cursor Radius 134
Cursor Tool 22,76
Curve Profile 89
Curve Tool 29,38,89,90
Curved Strokes 102
Custom Colors 49
Custom Icon 53
Custom Range 123
Customized Stroke 53
Customized Workspace 50
Customizing Brushes 52
Customizing Stroke Types 29
Customizing Strokes 47
Cutter Tool 26
Cutting Video Strips 60
Cycles 148

D

Data Properties 125
Datablock 59,96,93,121,132,141,185
Deleting 6
Depth and Resolution 100
Different Stroke Effects 88
Different Views 106
Dimensions Tab 151
Directories 175,177,178
Disk Drive 178

T

U

V